PRAISE FOR *THE STORMS OF LIFE*

K.J.'s book on suffering is honest, practical, and potent. It is so well written its strong medicine goes down well. When the weather in your life gets bad, it will encourage you and point you to the most powerful panacea in the Universe: the Lord God Almighty.

Sam R. Williams, Ph.D.
Professor of Counseling
Southeastern Baptist Theological Seminary

The Storms of Life is a practical guide that brings biblical clarity to chaos, wisdom to foolishness, and healing to the broken. It delivers a clear path to the One who rebukes the wind and says to the sea, "Peace! Be Still!"

Jeff Doyle, D-Min
Leadership Pastor
North Wake Church, Wake Forest, NC

The Storms of Life

Trusting God through Emotional Pains, Hurting Marriages, and Addictions

K. J. Nally

© Copyright 2014
By K. J. Nally
All Rights Reserved

Publishing by Rainer Publishing
www.rainerpublishing.com

ISBN 978-0692289396

The Holy Bible, English Standard Version® (ESV®)
Copyright © 2001 by Crossway,a publishing ministry of
Good News Publishers.
All rights reserved.

The Storms of Life

Trusting God through Emotional Pains, Hurting Marriages, and Addictions

K. J. Nally

DEDICATION

To all of you who have been shaken by the storms of life.

To my Sovereign Creator, who has given me many trials in my life to teach me wisdom and compassion. I hope you hear compassion, understanding, and wisdom in these coming pages—all a result of suffering.

And to my beloved, Dustin. You have comforted me in your strong arms too many times to count. Wrapped in your love, I get a glimpse of my glorious Savior.

"Trust is not a passive state of mind.
It is a vigorous act of the soul by which we choose to lay hold on the promises of God and cling to them despite the adversity that at times seeks to overwhelm us."

Trusting God: Even When Life Hurts by Jerry Bridges

Contents

Introduction	1
Chapter One: A Biblical Framework for Suffering	5

SECTION ONE: EMOTIONAL PAINS

Chapter Two: The Storm Hits	27
Chapter Three: Betrayal	49

SECTION TWO: HURTING MARRIAGES

Chapter Four: The Divorce Delusion	65
Chapter Five: Marital Mayhem	85

SECTION THREE: ADDICTIONS

Chapter Six: Addiction's Downward Spiral	103
Chapter Seven: Rebelling My Way	115
Chapter Eight: Fulfilled God's Way	127

SECTION FOUR: RESTORATION

Chapter Nine: The Power of Transformation	137
Chapter Ten: The Calmer of the Storm	145

INTRODUCTION

THE "S" WORD

Count it all joy, my brothers, when you meet trials of various kinds, for you know that the testing of your faith produces steadfastness.
James 1:2-3

I admit it. I am a struggling pessimist. *Well, God, here we go again. I won't get my hopes up just in case something doesn't turn out. That way if something bad happens, I half expected it, and if you surprise me with a blessing, I can get really excited.*

It's not a good thought process, and I'm certainly not the greatest woman of faith. For some, writing a book would seem the *impossible* feat. For me, it is discussing *suffering as a blessing*. Honestly, suffering was my least favorite topic of study. It became the "S" word. I became nervous when someone broached the topic of suffering. In some strange way, I was afraid that God allowed me to hear messages about the "S" word to prepare me for the next big boom. Perhaps I needed a "glass is half-full" pep talk from Winston Churchill who said, "A pessimist sees difficulty in every opportunity; an optimist sees opportunity in every difficulty." *God, grant me the wisdom to see the opportunity!*

In 2009, after much prayer, God confirmed that my husband and I were to move from Charleston, SC to attend Southeastern Baptist Theological Seminary. A growing passion to see marriages and families flourish put us on a journey to study biblical counseling. Our desire is to work in the church as a couple spurring on others to live a life radically transformed by the gospel of Christ. Before moving, our pastor in Charleston gave us this warning: "Prepare to suffer and have many trials once you arrive at seminary." He knew that the enemy would not be satisfied with us running after the Lord; he would try to destroy us through sin and suffering. He was right.

However, suffering is not at all like the suffering in my perceived fears. It is far worse and far sweeter than anything I have experienced in times of blessing. Even so, my heart yearns for blessing over suffering. I like comfort, health, and happiness. I have not yet arrived as the woman who embraces suffering with joy. Trust is still a daily battle. Joy is my prayer. But after walking through some burdensome trials, the Lord has allowed me to experience the God-given peace that comes through suffering and has given me compassion for those who suffer. *Suffering* is no longer a bad word, but a precious word that reminds me of my Savior and the love of my caring Father.

Many of you reading this book are suffering in a way that is heartbreaking and burdensome. I would image at times you feel as though you're drowning in the waves of your pain. Or you are reading because you are burdened for someone close to you who is suffering.

Scripture echoes our common plea in suffering: "Save me, O God! For the waters have come up to my neck. I sink in deep mire, where there is no foothold; I have come into deep waters, and the flood sweeps over me. I am weary with my crying out; my throat is parched. My eyes grow dim with waiting for my God" (Psalm 69:1-3). As a counselor, I would never offer quick advice to a counselee that sums up her problems or diminishes the struggle she is facing. Often, the journey of the trial teaches us more than even understanding it in hindsight, if God grants us that insight. In the same manner, we will journey together to understand suffering biblically and practically—and learn how to suffer well.

Modern psychologists tell us we need coping skills to *get through* life's crises. The Creator God who made us, however, explained that in Christ, we are "more than conquerors," victorious over trials and able to find joy even in the darkest times (Romans 8:37; James 1:1-12). With that truth, the following pages aren't simply a few coping methods to get you through, but hope for real change and lasting peace. Thankfully, there is a three-word conclusion that I hope you grasp by the last page: *God is sufficient*. No matter what you are facing, God is enough.

I realize the common reaction to suffering is fear or anger. Many people run from the Lord during times of suffering or create skewed ideas about the character of God. I've been there...I've done it too. This is a short book to be used as a personal study or as a counseling resource for someone who is in the midst of suffering.

The first chapter presents a biblical framework for understanding suffering. This chapter is brief because entire books have been written on this topic alone. I have included multiple resources on suffering for further reading in *Appendix A*. The following chapters briefly discuss common experiences of suffering: emotional pains, hurting marriages, and addictions. At the end of each chapter you will find a brief Bible study and practical application, either to be used as counseling homework for a counselee or as personal reflection. I would encourage you to read the book in its entirety, but if you can only read it in part, please read the first chapter defining suffering and finish with the section on restoration.

Scripture explains because of the "Father of mercies and God of all comfort, who comforts us in all our affliction . . . we may be able to comfort those who are in any affliction, with the comfort with which we ourselves are comforted by God" (2 Corinthians 1:3-4). May this short book be a comfort for your soul and encourage you to comfort others as we are tossed by the fiercest storms of life.

CHAPTER ONE

A BIBLICAL FRAMEWORK FOR SUFFERING

For I consider that the sufferings of this present time are not worth comparing with the glory that is to be revealed to us.
Romans 8:18

The Bible and life teach us that suffering comes in many forms. Suffering can come at the hand of someone who hurts you, causing bitterness and shame. It can be the self-inflicted consequences of sinful decisions, bringing regret and guilt. Suffering can be the result of living in a fallen world where sin reigns, bodies deteriorate, and natural disasters strike. Whether through tiresome trials, a shameful past, or battling sin, suffering comes to each of us. And it comes more often than we would like.

When bad things happen it is not because God is uncaring or unjust. He greatly loves us and desires more than our current happiness. God's goal for us is not solely contentment but also our transformation. God knows this life on earth is just a speck of time compared to eternity. He is most concerned about his glory displayed through our life and immortality. Counselor and professor, Sam Williams, explains, "Contentment is, or at least can be, a desirable biblical category. God's primary concern really is not our immortality in itself. It is his glory and our learning to enjoy it in all circumstances, which becomes even more important in view of our immortality—as all human beings live forever. God has set eternity into the hearts of men."

As Christians we are simply strangers on earth living in a world not our own, setting our eyes on the future grace to be given when we are with God—made perfect. And just as God asked Adam and Eve to trust him—even if they didn't understand everything He asked them to do—He asks us to trust him when we don't understand our circumstances. His promise to us is simple: He knows more than us, loves us, and desires our best (Isaiah. 55:8-9).

Trials Lead to Stronger Faith

God's Word clearly reveals that trials develop stronger faith in a true believer. James 1:2-4 encourages believers to "consider it pure joy, whenever we face trials of many kinds, because we know that the testing of our faith develops perseverance. Perseverance must finish its work so that you may be mature and complete, not lacking anything."

Yikes! Pure joy is not my gut response to suffering. I am learning that *this joy* looks differently than joy found in times of laughter and blessing. This joy is full of peace that surpasses our understanding. It causes us to humble ourselves under God's mighty hand, believing He will rescue us from drowning in our storm. It allows us to cast all our anxiety on him because He cares for us. It causes us to find genuine beauty in life because we know God is in control. And it makes us steadfast even when we want to give up! Sam Williams explains that "a theology of suffering gives us an immune system to understand. Then when it comes, we suffer well and do not question our faith."

So how do we develop a theology of suffering? We study and learn God's Word about his character, our sin nature, the world, and our eternity. Knowing truth about life, death, and eternity will enable us to keep a perspective when our world begins to quake.

The Enemy Desires Destruction

Beware! Scripture tells us beyond our own sin nature and natural disasters we must be self-controlled and alert because the enemy—the Devil—prowls around like a roaring lion looking for someone to devour. Resist him, we are told. We must stand firm in the faith, because the lion is after someone who is weak, alone, and unfocused. In that weak, trial-induced brokenness, God calls to us: *Trust Me! I will give you every ounce of strength you need to keep your focus on the eternal goal.*

Our promise in suffering is sure: The God of all grace, who called us to his eternal glory in Christ, after we have suffered a little while, will restore us and make us strong, firm, and steadfast! For all eternity, we will be completely restored, having no more pain (1 Peter 5:6-10; Revelation 21:4).

Victory in Suffering

What victory in overcoming trials! We must honestly ask ourselves which of these statements is most important: (1) Getting the most out of this worldly life through a lifestyle that seeks to satisfy my every desire, or (2) pursuing a life that even when I don't understand, chooses to trust God for life's fulfillment and joy for all eternity.

The first choice often results in anger toward God when trials strike, and the second choice results in praise toward God and joyful fulfillment even in the midst of trials. Whatever trial comes our way—sickness, death of a loved one, abuse, sin, financial strain—God gives us a reason not to fear. He says, "Neither death nor life, neither angels nor demons, neither the present nor the future, nor any powers, neither height nor depth, nor anything else in all creation, will be able to separate us from the love of God that is in Christ Jesus our Lord."[1] No matter the trial, whether sin or suffering, God's all-enduring love gives us hope.

Jerry Bridges explains that in order to trust God, we must always view our adverse circumstances through the eyes of faith. Just as faith of salvation comes through hearing the message of the gospel, so the faith to trust God in adversity comes through the Word of God.

In the area of adversity Scripture teaches us three essential truths about God—truths we must believe if we are to trust him.

1. God is completely sovereign (or in control).
2. God in infinite in wisdom.
3. God is perfect in love.
   God in his love always wills what is best for us. In his wisdom He always knows what is best, and in his sovereignty He has the power to bring it about. [2]

You may be wondering how your current struggle could be God's best. Or if God really loves you how He could be putting you through this trial. It's a logical question that my finite mind cannot answer, except to express; He promises in his Word that our trials are for our best and his glory because He loves us.

Suffering in the Old and New Testament

Hear these words from the servant God called the "man after my own heart:" "How long, O Lord? Will you forget me forever? How long will you hide your face from me? How long must I wrestle with my thoughts and every day have sorrow in my heart? How long will my enemy triumph over me? Look on me and answer, O Lord my God. Give light to my eyes, or I will sleep in death . . . But, I trust in your unfailing love; my heart rejoices in your salvation. I will sing to the Lord for he has been good to me" (David, Psalm 13).

Take a moment to read through a psalm of lament, such as Psalm 42. Like Psalm 13, they were written to express feelings of deep sorrow and abandonment from the Lord during a terrible trial. After expressing burdens and fears, the writer ends the lament with a claim to trust the Lord despite the circumstance.

Listen to another suffering servant of the Lord who admitted, "I pleaded with the Lord to [take away my thorn], But He said to me, 'My grace is sufficient for you, for my power is made perfect in weakness.' Therefore I will boast all the more gladly of my weaknesses, so that the power of Christ may rest upon me. For the sake of Christ, then, I am content with weaknesses, insults, hardships, persecutions, and calamities. For when I am weak, then I am strong."[3] Those words were said by Paul, writer of much of the New Testament. If you've read the New Testament you know this man *knew* suffering.

Both the New Testament and Old Testament are filled with real people with terrible struggles, doubts, and fears. Why would God allow this raw honesty to be written for generation after generation to read if not to show his compassionate understanding? Scripture declares you are not the only person facing such calamity and gives encouragement to share our emotions with others. Whether we choose to believe it or not, God never abandons his children. Suffering displays God's mercy and love!

It's War Time: Ammo Up!

The Bible is full of military terminology, because if you are breathing you're at war! Just as earthly combat must have a strategy when the enemy is attacking, military tactics are also undoubtedly needed during times of spiritual suffering. So, we must go to the Word, our ammo, to battle the assaults that come with suffering.

Paul says, "I consider that our present sufferings are not worth comparing with the glory that will be revealed in us. And we know that in all things God works for the good of those who love him, who have been called according to his purpose . . .What, then, shall we say in response to this? If God is for us, who can be against us? He who did not spare his own Son, but gave him up for us all—how will he not also, along with him, graciously give us all things?"[4] Do you realize that God always gives us the strength to get through every trial? Do you believe it? He never asks us to carry a burden alone. And quite honestly, he never asks us to carry our own burdens. Our Father asks us to allow him to carry our burdens, to give over control, and He will give the power to praise him through it.

When we focus on the cross of Christ—both his sacrifice for us and the power He fills us with to live for him—we can give God glory and show the watching world that our God is powerful and good even in painful circumstances. The author of *The Gospel Primer*, Milton Vincent explains it this way: "More than anything else could ever do, the gospel enables me to embrace my tribulations and thereby position myself to gain full benefit from them. For the gospel is the one great permanent circumstance . . . every hardship in my life is allowed by God only because it serves his gospel purpose in me. I realize that the gospel in not just one piece of good news that fits into my life somewhere among all the bad . . . the gospel makes genuinely good news out of every other aspect of my life, including my severest trials."[5]

Milton continues to explain that the good news of our trials is that God is forcing them to do the greatest good for us by conforming us to the image of Christ. Only then can we embrace trials as friends and allow them to do God's good work in us.

Cautions When Suffering

Caution One: It is easy to doubt God's love.

Suffering often reveals our heart's greatest desires. Think about it. When you don't get your way, do you get angry at God and believe He is not trustworthy? Not trusting God that He can be glorified by our current trial says we do not believe He loves us or will fight our battles. When we suffer our world starts to turn inward. It gets smaller and focused on self. We often lose perspective that we are part of a bigger story, God's story.

God tells us the secret to peace: "[I] will keep in perfect peace (Shalom) those whose minds are steadfast, because they trust in [me]. Trust in the LORD forever, for the LORD, the LORD himself, is the Rock eternal."[6] Trust! Our God knows that trusting him brings the greatest peace. And trust comes through believing in Jesus Christ as Savior. He fought our eternal battle and won! Therefore, finding fulfillment in Christ leads us to God's best and gives us the most joy. This is why it is so important to go back to the cross: God so loved the world He gave up his Son...for us. There is no doubt, God loves us and knows what is best to chisel us most like Jesus. Are you willing to be clay in the Potter's hands?

Caution Two: One of Satan's greatest schemes is isolation.

Satan desires to fool us into believing no one else can truly understand our pain, so we must deal with it alone. I will give more details in chapter two, but I experienced a trial when I began feeling like this—all alone. If we believe this lie, no one can encourage us or speak truth in our lives. We stop seeking help from others, we stop going to church, and we definitely stop reading God's Word. This process can lead us to the point where we believe Jesus, God himself, does not understand our suffering. *He was God, after all, He could handle it.* Then we become isolated, bitter, angry, and often depressed. Don't let Satan fool you into believing this lie.

The Foundation of Suffering

All of life is worship, and we worship either God or self in all of life's blessings and trials. Before we begin our discussion about specific topics of suffering, I want to encourage you take a look at your heart. Without the perspective of the cross of Jesus Christ and a God who is carrying your burdens, suffering cannot be done well.

We are part of a bigger story than our own pain. When we realize this truth we are transformed. It brings a perspective that we are not the only person experiencing pain and that God has bigger plans for our suffering. Let me bring you into the greatest story ever told.

Digesting the Story[7]

In my years spent as an English teacher I taught my students about the five elements of a story:

1. *Exposition*—the beginning of the story and introduction of the setting and characters
2. *Rising action*—the introduction of the problem or conflict
3. *Climax*—the high point, the moment of darkest fate and joyous rescue

4. *Falling action*—the crisis winds down and choices are made
5. *Resolution*—the conclusion of the story, conflicts are resolved, loose ends are tied up, and it concludes with a happy or sad ending

Often people approach the Bible as a reference book, a series of individual stories that are hard to make sense of together. The Word of God can be easily reduced to a book that answers how we are to live in various situations. Sounds boring! Sure, there is truth to this approach...it can be helpful, as we will see study suffering, but often it leads to a *me-centered* approach Bible reading.

Tullian Tchividjian explains the fallacy of this approach: "It is possible to read the Bible, study the Bible, memorize portions of the Bible and miss the whole point. In other words it is entirely possible to read the stories and miss the Story."[8]

The Bible, with its 66 books and 40 authors writing over a period of about 1,600 years, is one big story. It is the redemption story, which can be referred to as a metanarrative. This means it is a grand, all-encompassing story that gives an account of the historical record. The Bible provides a framework that your own experiences and thoughts can be structured.

The theme of this story is God's grace to us through Jesus' rescue of sinners and the redemption of the world. Every person on the earth is a participant in his Story. J.R.R. Tolkien argues that the Gospel of Jesus is the underlying reality to which all other stories point. The reason the story of Jesus in so powerful is that it is true.

The biblical narrative is broken into four acts: creation, fall, rescue, and restoration. This section is adapted from *The Story*,[9] an evangelistic guide used to share the truth of Jesus Christ. Now, enter into God's story of creation, incarnation, and restoration—find your part—and experience your history and future with a renewed purpose.

The Creation

"In the beginning, God created the heavens and the earth." Genesis 1:1

Like a painting on a canvas, the narrative begins. Stroke by stroke, the picture is coming to life. Chapter one of Genesis is an introduction like no other, it is the dawning of creation, the moment God made the earth and every living thing. The first two chapters introduce all God has created, his most treasured creation (humanity), and where they are to worship him forever. Welcome to the exposition. We learn from these chapters that God is the main character of the story. He is eternal. He is one God in three persons. He is holy and righteous. He is love. He deserves glory! God's creation was to live together with him in perfect harmony, so they were flourishing.

The Fall

"So when the woman saw that the tree was good for food, and that it was a delight to the eyes, and that the tree was to be desired to make one wise, she took of its fruit and ate, and she also gave some to her husband who was with her, and he ate." Genesis 3:6

We can look around us and know something is not right in this world. Wars, famines, children dying, murders, adultery, hatred...it is broken. In Genesis 3 we meet the serpent who is there to entice Adam and Eve to rebel against this loving, good God. The action is rising. Satan's leading question and lie causes Eve to make a reconsideration of her whole life. He said to the woman, "Did God actually say, 'You shall not eat of any tree in the garden'?" Satan misquoted the command in Genesis 2:16-17 reducing the lavish generosity of God to the level of withholding good gifts.

This single rule from God would test Adam and Eve's loyalty and trust in their Creator. With these deceptive words of Satan, the Garden doesn't look quite the same to Eve. The tree of good and evil is now the forbidden center of her world, making this command grow more severe. Pride begins to bud. In that moment, Eve not only doubted God's goodness (or that He would deliver such severe consequences), she also believed she should be like God, knowing everything. God's threat of death is toned down by Eve. She does not repeat God's warning to the serpent, "If any eat of it you shall surely die." Instead she says you should not touch it or eat it "lest you die." God's warning said, "You will certainly, absolutely die…make no mistake about it!" The word Eve used, "lest," means the possibility of something undesirable happening. In other words, there may be some disagreeable consequences, but compared to the pleasures of the moment, they're not bad enough to discourage you from indulging in disobedience.

This is the same lie Satan continues to deceive us with! In that moment, Eve not only doubted God's goodness, she also doubted that God would deliver such severe consequences. I fear we are Eve's daughters. Consequences will never be enough to drive obedience; only love is strong enough. We must believe the truth that God really does want our best and will deliver it in his way and time.

In rebellion, Adam and Eve decided that they, not God, would determine what is right and what is wrong. Sin had entered the world through every human heart by this choice to distrust the God who fashioned them. Romans explains, "Just as sin came into the world through one man, and death through sin, and so death spread to all men because all sinned."[10] The consequence of sin is destroyed harmony. Instead of peace with God, we're rebels on the run. Instead of harmony with creation, we break and destroy creation. And instead of intimacy with God and others, we have dysfunctional relationships. We are broken spiritually, physically, socially, emotionally, and morally. The crisis has occurred: Sin has caused eternal separation from the God of creation and suffering has begun.

The Rescue

"And I will put enmity between you and the woman, and between your offspring and hers; he will crush your head, and you will strike his heel." Genesis 3:15

When I get to this part of the story, my heart begins beating faster. Why are our hearts so enamored with the idea of a hero? Superman, Batman, Thor, Spiderman, Hercules, and basically every book and movie ever made—they each have some kind of hero, a savior.

But this isn't just some story. This is the story of life. In the moment of utter despair when all hope seemed lost for all eternity, God rescued us from darkness and brought us into the kingdom of the Son He loves! This is the height of action when the darkest moment turns to joyous rescue!

Only a few verses after Eve chose to eat from the tree of good and evil, God explains that though sin will physically kill man, the serpent's head will be forever crushed. He has a plan of salvation for his beloved people. Sin had to be dealt with, for its penalty required payment from the sinner. According to Scripture, it required death. As humanity suffered from the consequences of sin, the God of creation wrote himself into the story to rescue all that had been lost.

About 600 years before Jesus, God spoke to Jeremiah saying, "I will give them singleness of heart and action...I will make an everlasting covenant with them: I will never stop doing good to them, and I will inspire them to fear me, so that they will never turn away from me."[11] God the Son, named Jesus Christ, is introduced as the Hero—our Savior.

The inspiration we need was God coming in the form of a man to rescue us from the bonds of sin and death (Jesus is 100% God and 100% man). Jesus lived the sinless life we could not. He perfectly fulfilled the law of God. He came to earth willingly, obediently, and sufficiently to suffer and die for sin. Jesus died the death we should have died, paying the price for our sins.

First Peter tells us that Christ "suffered once for sins, the righteous for the unrighteous, that he might bring us to God."[12] But Jesus didn't just die for sin, He rose from the dead and returned to the Father! "In his death, the perfect blood of Jesus—holy God and innocent Man—was spilled. His sacrifice provided the permanent covering for sin, forever conquering its grip on the souls of men and the wonder of creation."[13]

When we turn to the Rescuer, who offered the ultimate act of worship and obedience to the Father, we are set free to worship and obey God as He originally designed. In Christ, perfect love drives out all fear. We are set free by the true Hero!

Restoration

"Behold, I am making all things new." Revelation 21:5

The Rescuer has come. The enemy is defeated. Choices must be made. Those who have put their trust in Jesus Christ as their substitute will experience the fullness of the gift of his sacrifice.

When God makes all things new, those children of God will be with him forever! These children will also be sinless, loving God and others perfectly. Humanity and creation will be made new (Romans 8:19-21). We will be restored spiritually, physically, socially, emotionally, and morally. God also promises a new heaven and earth, so the brokenness of this world will also be redeemed. The disunity and pain brought by disobedience and sin will be forever restored so that we will have perfect harmony and intimacy with our creator God. Truly this will be fulfilled with Christ's return.

For now, if we have been called by God to know Jesus, then we have the promise that "His divine power has given us everything we need for life and godliness."[14] Because of the resurrection power of Christ rising from the dead, conquering sin, God guides us with the power of the Holy Spirit to live a victorious holy life. In this life temptations will come, and at times sin will be embraced. But God promises, "Though you may stumble, you will not fall, for the LORD upholds you with his hand."[15] We will never be abandoned by God because He sees Christ when He looks at us!

Saved by Christ

We were made to live with God in heaven. Everyone on earth is here purposefully created by God to seek him and personally know him (Acts 17:24-27). Do you realize that everyone you walk by is an immortal being? God gives all humanity the choice to accept him or reject him, and all men either fulfill or forsake their chief purpose.

Many people have confused salvation in Jesus to be a single moment in life where you prayed for him to be Savior of your life, giving no thought to his Lordship. Many may call themselves Christians, yet they do not truly know Jesus as Savior and Lord. Understand that is God's grace that saves us—it's nothing we do. But Scripture does teach that to be saved you must "confess with your mouth that Jesus is Lord and believe in your heart that God raised him from the dead, then you will be saved. For with the heart one believes and is justified, and with the mouth one confesses and is saved."[16]

The knowledge of who Jesus is as Savior God is foundational to belief, but a relinquishing of self for the Savior's lordship is necessary for salvation. God desires true belief and total surrender. Realize that total surrender comes more fully as the Holy Spirit trains and teaches you.

Do you know him as your Savior and Lord? If you aren't certain, take some time now to meet with the One who created you to be his child. There is no good way to overcome addiction, hurt, or battle suffering without the Rock, Jesus, giving us a foundation to prevail and a purpose to reveal. Ask Jesus to forgive your sins, acknowledge that He is the Savior of humanity, and give him your life to lead as He desires. God, through the Holy Spirit, often uses the Bible, prayer, other believers, and life experiences to mold us into his image.

We are about to begin a study that challenges you through the Word, encourages you to have a deep relationship with God, and shares experiences to help you apply the truth. God is sufficient, even in your suffering. Now let's begin this important journey.

Biblical Study and Practical Application

1. Get a prayer journal to write in during this study. Write out your sufferings. As you write, pray to God. Remember He is sufficient, even during times of suffering.

2. Write your own lament. Include a cry to the Lord, the problem (fears, frustration, burden, etc.), and finish with a claim of trust to the Lord.

3. Choose a Psalm of Lament that explains how you are feeling. See *Appendix B* for *Using Scripture to Express Great Grief.*

4. Write down all the blessings you have on a daily basis. Keep a log so you can flip back through when having a day of burden in your trial.

5. Go outside to experience creation. Sit with God and share your heart with him. You may want to record this in a prayer journal.

6. Read Romans 8:28-32 and 2 Corinthians 1:3-4. What reasons does God allow us to go through trial?

7. Answer questions in *Appendix C*: *Identity Study: A Few Brief Questions to See Your Heart.*

Section One: Emotional Pains

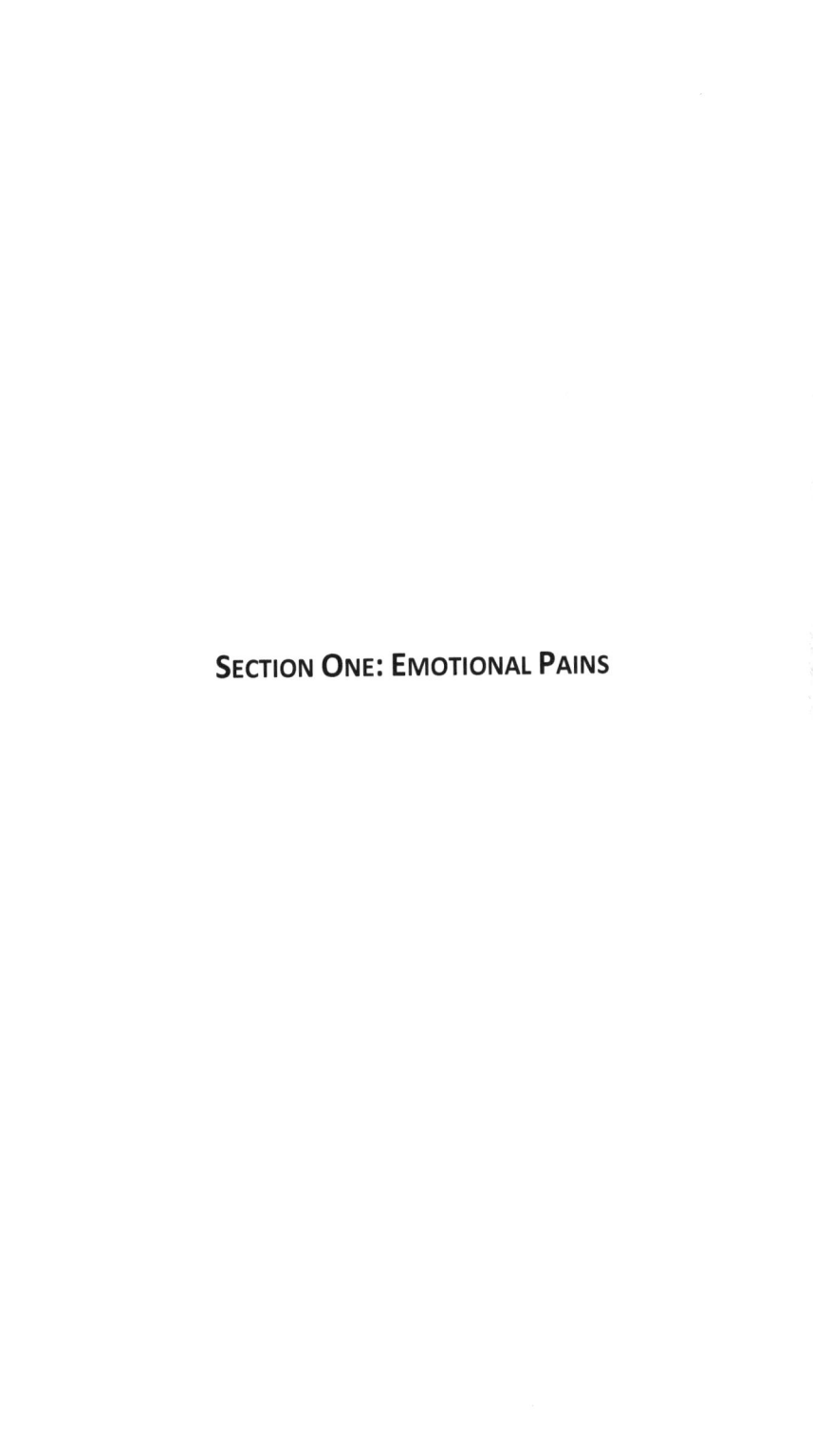

Chapter Two

The Storm Hits

When my heart was grieved and my spirit embittered, I was senseless and ignorant; I was a brute beast before you. Yet I am always with you; you hold me by my right hand. You guide me with your counsel, and afterward you will take me into glory. Whom have I in heaven but you? And earth has nothing I desire besides you. My flesh and my heart may fail, but God is the strength of my heart and my portion forever.
Psalm 73:21-26

Every month was a physical reminder of what happened. Every month my emotions warred against my heart and what I knew to be truth. Why wasn't this easier? And why did each month seem to force me on an emotional rollercoaster? I felt God's presence in midst of the storm...why did He seem so far off now? I know He is beside me, guiding me, holding me up by my right arm. His Word promises He never leaves. He always seeks his glory and the good of those who love him. Yes, I know that is truth . . . help me Lord to believe it.

These words from Psalm 73 are a salve to the broken soul.

If you're human, then you have stories of suffering to share. The New Testament writers tell us we will *all* suffer in *various* ways. Over the next few pages I will share with you one of my stories of suffering. I do not elevate this as the ultimate story of suffering, nor do I diminish it as not as difficult to bear as another's story. Just as the trial you are currently going through weakens your heart and leaves tear-stained cheeks, every moment of suffering is significant. You don't have to relate to this particular situation to understand emotional pain. It is simply an example of one of the "various trials" the Lord has allowed my husband and I to experience for our good and his glory...and we are still in the midst of it.

A Decision to Give Up Control

After three years of marriage, my husband, Dustin, and I decided to go off all forms of contraception. Having personal convictions about using a birth control pill, we decided while driving to visit family in Pigeon Forge that I would toss my remaining pills in the trash. I have often struggled with the sin of control (i.e. distrust of God's best) so we decided it was most glorifying to God for us to give up the façade. It would be God's timing to expand our family. We surrendered and waited excitedly for God to bless us with a baby.

One year and three months passed—still no baby. Thoughts of infertility started rising. My gynecologist suggested tests and possible fertility medication. We were only 26. We weren't opposed to medication, but I wasn't ready to go down that road. We prayed for God's blessing of a child. During that time an emotional game of tug-of-war pulled to overthrow my contentment. Many friends announced the news of their pregnancies. With excitement I congratulated them, but once in the solitude of my home, I wept softly from the fears and brokenness lodged in my own heart.

Winter had settled in and we celebrated our fourth anniversary. Our hearts were content waiting on the Lord. Still emotions teetered to steal our peace. Busy with work, church, counseling, and school Dustin and I rarely got a date night out. One Thursday on a cool January evening we planned a special dinner date, because we finally had the night off and a $25 gift card for Outback. For the last couple of weeks I was feeling strange, I was moody and there was a dull ache on my left side. I called my doctor fearing I had another ovarian cyst. They told me if the pain wasn't severe that I didn't need to come in immediately, but to take a pregnancy test in a few days.

Thursday Date Night

Dustin would be home from work any minute. I rushed around the house getting ready for our date night. I heard his truck pull in the drive way, my heart was pounding in my chest. We greeted each other with a kiss and I grabbed his briefcase as he went into the bedroom to change into jeans before we left. Since he was tired from a long day at work, I offered to drive to dinner. As we chatted in the truck about the day, instead of driving to the restaurant I parked the truck at the seminary and asked Dustin to follow me. "I have a little surprise for you," I said as I took his hand and led him along the sidewalk leading to the mission's building on campus. We stood in the center of the building, surrounded by stained glass pictures of people from all around the world impacted by the gospel of Jesus Christ. "Yesterday you told me your mission's professor said, 'Missions begins in the home and goes out from there,'" I recalled to Dustin. "Well, I have something for you." I handed Dustin a paper that read:

> *Once upon a time there was a beautiful lady . . .*
> *And a handsome gentleman.*
> *They went away on a weekend getaway that was filled with fun and love. Yes, they loved each other very passionately indeed!*
>
> *Dustin, I was thinking of ways to make this night very special for you. You are my favorite! You are everything I could ever ask for in a husband . . . you are my immeasurably more. What a godly husband you are, and I know, will continue to grow into.*
>
> *It seems though, in my plans to make tonight special to show you how much I love you, God had different plans...*

When I told you earlier today I had a surprise for you, you said… "It better be something very small."

Please open part one of your surprise…the rest of the gift will come later.

And they all lived Happily Ever After!

As Dustin opened his gift that was wrapped in layers of green tissue paper, he asked excitedly, "Did you plan for us to go on a mission trip!" He opened it and starred. It was my positive pregnancy test. We stood there hugging and crying. We were thrilled. The surprise was very small indeed. We were going to have a baby! He was so small we called him our Lil' Bean.

The Story of Lil' Bean

Nine weeks went by and I was feeling so good. We joked that maybe there wasn't a baby in my "belly" because I didn't feel pregnant. Sure, I was tired and ate everything in sight, but I felt great. Excitedly, we arrived at the doctor . . .it would be Lil' Bean's first picture (medically they term it *ultrasound*, but I like *first picture* better!). As we sat in the room waiting for the doctor, we gave each other a high five and then pumped the air three times toward heaven, giving God three high fives because this was his perfect work, not ours. We had determined from the first day God blessed us with our baby to have "open hands." This was God's little one, entrusted to us to raise him to be a worshiper of God. The doctor came in and talked for some time about what to expect and hospital protocol—then it was time for "baby's first picture."

Silence. This isn't what an ultrasound was supposed to look like, I thought. Where was my baby? The picture was white with only a small black circle. No heartbeat. The doctor didn't need to say anything; we knew. And our hearts broke. The doctor left the room after a short explanation of what would happen over the next few days. She told me not to blame myself. But in that moment as my world spun out of control, I couldn't stop the thoughts. I wept in my husband's strong arms. Slowly I met his gaze and said, "I'm so sorry. I'm so sorry." He knew what I meant and gently held my tear stained face. "Don't you dare go there," he softly warned. "Don't you dare take credit for what God is doing." I knew the truth. God was in control, He was faithful, and He was good. But could I believe that in this moment?

On Sunday, October 2, 2011 it would have been our little baby's due date. When we lost our baby, we cried to the point of exhaustion. It was so sweet falling in love with our first child. It gave us a small glimpse of how God loves us and how his heart must break when people die before knowing their Father, miscarried for eternity.

THE STORM HITS

The day after we lost our baby, I prayed to God for strength to praise him even when I hurt so deeply. I have never felt the nearness of my Lord like I did in the midst of this pain. In those moments I was a fragile little girl rocking back and forth in a heap on her bedroom floor, crying with no more strength to give—I needed my Father. I know that while I rocked the Father's arms tightly held me. Even when I felt emotionally drained and spiritually broken the months that followed, He gave me the strength to praise him even through the pain. This is my prayer to God the day after I lost my Lil' Bean.

My Good God,

> Thank you for the love and strength you've given me over the last two days. You have wrapped Dustin and me in your compassionate embrace. Lord, this is so hard. This baby you gave us was such a gift. We never tried taking credit for him or even desired control. It seems sometimes the purest, most special things you take away. And that is okay. My God, as hard as losing my perfect little baby has been, I know your plan is best. I am no longer pregnant nor have a little life growing in my womb...I am no longer a mommy-to-be. This is so hard. Seeing my incredible, strong husband crumble with brokenness is so hard. My Lord, we really fell in love with our baby just eight

weeks old. Thank you for sustaining us through the horrific time of seeing him and for the gift of getting to see him and pray over him as we said 'goodbye.' Goodbye came so much faster than we could ever have imagined. I never expected this...it was such a gift. I am broken Lord, but your Word is so true...you are close to the brokenhearted. We feel you...and you are good.

Lord it breaks my heart I will never get to meet my child. I will never get to watch him grow. I will never get to hold him or tell him how much I love him. I never got to name him. But the truth of your Word is that he is loved now more than Dustin and I ever could. He got to meet you, his perfect Father. You got to embrace him with your comforting arms. He will never know the sorrows and pain of this sinful world. He is with you forever! And instead of us watching him grow, he will watch his mom and his dad grow in maturity, in Christ-likeness, while we're here on this earth. And one day You will allow us the meeting we never got here on earth. We will call him by the name You gave him!

Lord, I can't help but think, as Dustin said to me yesterday that this pain we feel is small in comparison to the pain you feel daily. Daily watching men and women die never meeting their Father. Never getting to be born as a new man into Your family. Never feeling the embrace of their Father's love. Never being named . . .Child of God. And Lord . . .that is for eternity. Our pain ends with this earthly existence.

Forgive me for being so focused on this life. You have blessed Dustin and me in so many ways. Trials and suffering are part of this sinful existence (James 1), but Lord how you make my heart soar even when I can barely lift my head. Joy does come in the morning! Lord, your Word says because of your great love we are not consumed. For your compassions never fail. They are new every morning; great is your faithfulness. And I say, "My flesh and my heart may fail, but God is the strength of my heart and my portion forever. You are my portion; therefore I will wait for you" (Lamentations 3:22-24, Psalm 73:26).

Lord, great is your faithfulness. Though we don't understand any of this—and we won't try to either—we know your mercies are great and your ways are best. Please help Dustin and me to wait on you. Let not the fears of the future take hold of our hearts. Where would we be if we didn't have You? O Lord, how could one survive this life without You? Dustin and I realized again yesterday how life is only able to be lived with You in it. Please burden the hearts of our lost friends and family members. Allow our pain to soften their hearts to see their need for their Savior. Let them not die apart from knowing their Father's loving embrace. This has changed our lives and we pray it changes others lives in an eternal way. Lord, please continue to heal my body. And Lord, please continue to heal our hearts. You are so good my God. Jesus, thank you for dying for my sins so that I would have the chance to *know* my Father. And thank you for rising from the dead, conquering death so that I can *be with* my Father for all eternity. May Dustin and I give you all glory and praise every day of our lives, even in times of utter despair. Thank you Lord…your way is much better than mine.

I love you,

Your child (Kori Jo)

The Emotional Rollercoaster

On Friday February 25, 2011 we got to see our baby, pray over him, and say, "Good bye." The confusion and pain that filled my heart was suffocating. Why would God bless us in such an incredible way only take it away so quickly? But just as the pain threatened to steal my trust in the Lord, God was so near and filled me with the most unexplainable peace and strength. By no means do I mean that I was super-spiritual, quickly recovered from the pain, or even to this day understand this trial, but I can give praise to the Lord. I was grounded in his truth, the Bible, and He did fill me with inexpressible joy during the loss. Through my suffering, He taught me so many lessons from his Word, and I got to share with hundreds of people the good news of Jesus Christ.

Over three years later, we still have moments of sadness of what could have been, but we must remind ourselves of truth. The truth is that God is *good*. He is in absolute control for his glory and our best. We praise the Lord we got to experience the joy of finding out we were going to be parents. We experienced the dreams of a growing family. And even if only for a short time, I got to experience what is was like to be pregnant: highly emotional, strange dreams, going to the bathroom 52 times a day, and eating every five minutes!

But, it was short . . .too short. Every month is a challenge to trust in the Lord's best and perfect timing. We cling to the truth of who God is—our loving Father who cherishes us so much He would give his *only son* to die in our place so that we could be grafted into his Family. He is our strong provider. Even though we may not understand why having a baby is not best for us now, He knows and is giving us exactly what we need for this time.

The well-known and cherished passage helps in times of disbelief and lack of understanding: "For my thoughts are not your thoughts, neither are your ways my ways, declares the Lord. For as the heavens are higher than the earth, so are my ways higher than your ways and my thoughts than your thoughts" (Isaiah 55:8-9). My husband and I are still waiting for the Lord to bless us with children and the gift of being parents. It certainly isn't our fleshly default, but we continue to trust the Creator of Life.

Lessons Learned in Trust

One of my favorite books during this trial was Jerry Bridges' *Trusting God: Even When Life Hurts*. Bridges sums up his book by saying, "[For many of us] obeying God makes sense to us. In most cases, his laws appear reasonable and wise, and even when we don't want to obey them, we usually concede that they are good for us. But the circumstances we find ourselves in often defy explanation. When unexpected situations arise that appear unjust, irrational, or even dreadful, we feel confused and frustrated. And before long, we begin to doubt God's concern for us or his control over our lives."[17] As mentioned earlier, adversity is hard to endure, and at times, even harder to understand.

It all comes down to trust. Can we trust God to love us always? Can we trust God to make the best choices for our lives? Can we trust God even when there is no explanation for the events unfolding in our lives? Can we trust that God is both loving and sovereign . . . all the time? Can we trust that every step of our lives is a means to bring glory to God? Can we trust God is controlling these events for our good . . .

even if we never see the 'good' in our lifetime (Romans 8:38-39)?

This has been my journey. These questions were (and are) my questions. In trials of infertility, miscarriage, sin, finances, and serious health concerns, would I *choose* to trust the truth of God's character or my own devastated feelings?

A Story of Trust

A woman now worshiping at the feet of Jesus gave me hope. She never knew me, but her song resonates truth in my heart. You may know of William J. Kirkpatrick who wrote the music to *'Tis So Sweet to Trust in Jesus*. However, it was Louisa Stead who wrote the lyrics of this beloved hymn.

Louisa believed in the precious hope of Jesus' perfect work in her life and the sovereignty of God in terrible circumstances. In 1875, Louisa married. On one sunny afternoon, Louisa, her husband, and her daughter Lily, decided to go for a picnic. As the story goes, they enjoyed a picnic on Long Island Sound. Moments later, the Stead's heard a scream from a young boy drowning. Mr. Stead ran to the rescue, but tragically, Louisa watched helplessly as her beloved husband and the boy drowned. It is believed that Louisa wrote the lyrics for *'Tis So Sweet to Trust in Jesus* shortly after her husband's death. May our hearts echo her prayer of trust.

'Tis so sweet to trust in Jesus,
   And to take Him at his Word;
   Just to rest upon his promise,
   And to know, "Thus says the Lord!"

Jesus, Jesus, how I trust Him!
   How I've proved Him o'er and o'er
   Jesus, Jesus, precious Jesus!
   O for grace to trust Him more!

O how sweet to trust in Jesus,
   Just to trust his cleansing blood;
   And in simple faith to plunge me
   'Neath the healing, cleansing flood!

Yes, 'tis sweet to trust in Jesus,
   Just from sin and self to cease;
   Just from Jesus simply taking
   Life and rest, and joy and peace.

I'm so glad I learned to trust Thee,
   Precious Jesus, Savior, Friend;
   And I know that Thou art with me,
   Wilt be with me to the end.

Understanding Emotional Pain

Pain-filled emotion isn't innately bad. It's just not always trustworthy. Emotion is given to us from God to express life. But just as our age and sickness erode our physical bodies, and sin wages war against our spiritual bodies, our emotion is equally under the curse. It is fallen, so we can't blindly trust our emotion as the truth on which to base our decisions. Jeremiah 17 explains that the heart is deceitful above all things and desperately sick. We can't understand everything about our heart, feelings, or emotions.

Physical Trials

All emotional trials are terrible, but it seems some of the hardest trials can be those that affect us physically. Remember Job? After he lost property, wealth, and all his children, Satan hoped the last "straw" to break him was a physical disease that would ravage his body. Satan replied to God, "A man will give all he has for his own life. But now stretch out your hand and strike his flesh and bones, and he will surely curse you to your face."[18] We are created as both physical and spiritual beings. Our physical status affects our emotional and spiritual states. Therefore, physical illness can quickly strip us of joy because of the constancy and pain that consumes us.

Worry, a Great Enemy

As trials hit, worry is normally our initial response. Certainly, there are times when the fears of the unknown entice us to worry. Though I admit this with a proper amount of shame—I'm a seasoned worrier! Worry has actually caused physical ailments in my life: nausea, stomach pain, acid reflux, fatigue, heart palpitations, and anxiety. Scripture is very clear that God's children are not to worry about their lives, down to the minutest detail of clothing. Why? Our God is in control. He loves us, provides for us as He sees best, and has all our days ordained for us. What does worrying add to our life? I'll tell you . . . heart burn! Guard your heart and keep your thoughts away from worry. If necessary, as with any stronghold, form a battle plan against this sin if you struggle as I do.

No matter the source of the emotional pain, whether spiritual or physical, we must rely on the One who is in control and knows what we need for our best. Remember, our best is bringing God glory and being made into his image. So, in the midst of emotional pain we must constantly go back to the truth—my trials are making me more like Jesus for the glory of God! I repeat: *Your trials are making you more like Jesus for the glory of God.* We may state that we have faith in Jesus Christ as Sovereign Lord, but do we trust him enough to surrender our pains, suffering, families, and very lives? John Wesley said, "One of the greatest evidences of God's love to those that love him is to send them afflictions, with grace to bear them."[19]

We Live for More

If this world is the only thing we have, then suffering has no value. Life then is meaningless.

However, if the world is not our eternal home, then suffering must be viewed as purposeful in light of a future hope and home. The best thing you can do is know God intimately before a trial hits. Seek to understand the chaotic frailty of this life and the fulfilling eternality of our future home. Are you living your life on earth believing it should be a heaven-like experience? Christian, you aren't home yet!

Now on earth, the Lord has work to do in you and in others as they watch you. Do not blame God or turn from him in anger, but cling to the one who died for you so that He can comfort you as his son or daughter. David said in Psalm 90:10, "Those who know your name will trust in you, for you, Lord, have never forsaken those who seek you." Seek him friends . . .trust him . . . see that He is good, even (and especially) in times of pain.

If you are reading this book as an attempt to figure out God's character or find a reason for your pain because you don't know God personally, then what a great place to begin. Many times our darkest moments bring us closest to the Savior. We see in our brokenness that we can't do life on our own. Nor are we capable of stopping emotional hurts from happening. We must see our need for a Savior; one who will one day make all things right. So allow your suffering to lead you to the God who knows pain personally, can carry your burden, and will eventually take all suffering away. John 16:33 says, "I have told you these things, so that in me you may have peace. In this world you will have trouble. But take heart! I have overcome the world."

Give Up Control

I have found the harder I try to control my circumstance, the more anxious and distrusting I become. There is absolutely nothing we can physically or practically do in many circumstances we find ourselves in, but for some reason I try to analyze the situation and formulate possible outcomes. Often these outcomes are far bleaker than reality. They also leave me filled with fear. Therefore, the best action is to take captive your thoughts! Any sinful, distrusting thought that enters your mind—whether lust because your desire to marry is still unfulfilled or fear because a large tumor is found in your body—you are instructed to take captive all thoughts that set themselves up against the truth and make them obedient to Christ (2 Corinthians 10:3-5).

Keep an eternal perspective, because your Father who fashioned you in your mother's womb loves you. Nothing you do or don't do determines God's love for you. He asks you to trust him and give him worship in every stage and circumstance of life. Remember the cross. God's unfailing love for us is "an objective fact affirmed over and over in the Scriptures. It is true whether we believe it or not. Our doubts do not destroy God's love, nor does our faith create it. It originates in the very nature of God, who is love, and it flows to us through our union with his beloved Son." [20] In the emotional pain you are currently in, trust that God has bigger plans for this suffering, that He loves you, and desires your best. Take action to *choose* to trust him by preaching the gospel to yourself daily, captivating your thoughts, surrounding yourself with encouraging Christians, and resting in his Word.

These words from J. C. Ryle have brought me much encouragement: "Reader, if God has given you his only begotten Son, beware of doubting his kindness and love, in any painful providence of your daily life! Never allow yourself to think hard thoughts of God. Never suppose that He can give you anything which is not really for your good…See in every sorrow and trouble of your earthly pilgrimage the hand of Him who gave Christ to die for your sins! Say to yourself in the darkest hour of trial, 'This also is ordered by Him who gave Christ to die for my sins. It cannot be wrong. It is done in love. It must be well.'"[21]

Biblical Study and Practical Application

1. When God seems far how do we continue holding onto our faith? We must *trust*. Study these passages about God's character. Journal about the verses, including what verses mean the most to you and why.
    - Trust that God is true and his Word is truth (Psalm 53:1; Colossians 1:15-23; 1 Timothy 3:16-17; Hebrews 4:12).

- Trust that God loves his children more than we can fathom (1 John 3:1; 1 John 4:19; Romans 8:38-39).
- Trust that God wants the best for us, just as any parent does on earth...though He is much wiser (Romans 8:28-30; 2 Peter 1:2-10; Jeremiah 17:8).
- Trust that God's way brings him the most glory (Psalm 19:1; Psalm 108:4-6; Luke 2:14).
- Trust that God never leaves us alone in pain, but He holds our hand and walks with us (Psalm 90:10; Deuteronomy 31:6; Hebrews 13:5).
- Trust that God will one day take all pain away when we are with him in eternity (John 16:33; John 10:10; Revelation 21:4).
- Trust that God is good *all* the time! (Psalm 84; Psalm 73:1; Mark 10:18).

2. Spend a day or half-day in solitude with the Lord. Go to a place that is quiet, beautiful, and where you can be alone. Do not bring anything but your Bible and a journal. Listen to the Lord. Pray his Word. Take your thoughts captive (2 Corinthians 10:3-5). Share your fears but replace them with truth found in his Word. Take a nap or rest your eyes. Cry to the Lord for

mercy. Rest in the Psalms, hearing similar emotions and the resolve to trust the Lord. Finish your time choosing to trust the Lord.

3. Often when we are depressed by our circumstances and our thoughts are disobediently running wild, we feel focused on ourselves. To get out of a me-centered world, spend time during the week serving another person. You could write notes, plan a coffee date to talk about how they are doing, run an errand for your friend, counsel someone in need of hearing biblical truth, or just listen to someone who needs a friend.

4. Make a trust document: (1) Write down a prayer to God about how you are currently feeling with your fears. (2) List and explain each area of distrust and how you want the Lord to answer. (3) Pray specifically about each fear, releasing the outcome to God because of the truth you learned above in assignment one (include Scripture verses in your document so you can go back to them when you struggle).

5. Memorize Psalm 31:7-8 and Isaiah 26:3-4.

CHAPTER THREE

BETRAYAL

Make every effort to live in peace with everyone and to be holy; without holiness no one will see the Lord. See to it that no one falls short of the grace of God and that no bitter root grows up to cause trouble and defile many.
Hebrews 12:14-15

What if someone has victimized you—raped, abused, or persecuted you? You've been sinned against grievously. In the moments of utter shame or betrayal, God gives us great hope even in the midst of such a tragedy.

God Is the Battle Fighter

God tells us explicitly that when his children are mistreated he will fight the battle for them...and win! "It is mine to avenge; I will repay" (Romans 12:19). We are told to "be still before the Lord and wait patiently for him; not to fret when men succeed in their ways, when they carry out their wicked schemes. We are to refrain from anger and turn from wrath; for evil men will be cut off, but those who hope in the Lord will inherit the land."[22]

When my husband and I served with a Christ-centered addictions ministry where I was the director of women's ministry, my job was to minister to women who had been betrayed in the most terrible ways through their husband's ongoing addiction. I walked daily with them through their struggles. I counseled women who were suffering, ministering to wives who have been repeatedly betrayed by their husbands—a devastating consequence of an all-consuming addiction. I saw the results of the great lie of addiction: "My secret sins are only hurting me." The truth is the consequences of engaging in life-dominating sin bring destruction to the addicts, to their families, and to others who love them. When I counsel a wife who has been betrayed, I gently take her to the foot of the cross.

Learning Forgiveness

Wounded hearts are healed at the foot of the cross. Only there will you learn true forgiveness. Forgiveness is not something easily granted to a spouse who has broken the sweet vulnerability of the one-flesh marital unit. But forgiveness is commanded by God, and it is freeing. When the gospel of Jesus impacts our lives, forgiveness is not an option but an obligation in these bitter times. Forgiveness is the first big step in the long process of rebuilt trust.

Though I have worked with teens and single women as well, there is no more vulnerable relationship on earth than between a husband and wife. It often demonstrates the most difficult cases of betrayal and forgiveness. As we discuss forgiveness and even your sin, I want to be very careful you understand that even if you have failed in some way, your actions did not force your spouse to act sinfully.

The Great Equalizer

One of the hardest obstacles for an offended spouse is forgiving the enormity of the sins committed against you—compared to your *lesser* offenses. There is some truth here. The consequences of your spouse's sins have nearly destroyed you. And you may begin viewing your sins as a response to your spouse's *big* sins: anger, bitterness, control, manipulation, pride, self-righteousness, a hurtful tongue, and withholding forgiveness. That is why the cross of Jesus Christ is so important in these moments—it is the great equalizer. Sin has different worldly consequences, but all sin hardens our hearts toward God and others.

From Scripture we read, "*All* have sinned and fallen short of the glory of God."[23] The reason the cross is so magnificent is because *all* sinners are justified freely by his grace. If you are suffering with an addicted loved one, you may feel like these offenses are rarely even noticed by the one causing so much pain. *Does he even know what he is putting me through?* Remember Romans 5:8, Jesus suffered and died for us while we were . . . over and over . . . betraying and offending God. We were his enemies. Jesus laid his life down for you and me *as a sacrifice* so He would free enslaved sinners.

We did to Jesus exactly what your loved one enslaved to an addiction is doing to you—except Jesus suffered unto death and he was perfect in every action, word, and thought. We all are sinners and most of us would readily admit that. But when someone has offended you, especially an offense that is repeated over and over again, it is hard to see past the pain.

In chapter seven we will discuss the suffering of someone paralyzed by sin's grasp (i.e. addiction) and how to find freedom. But for the one sinned against, true forgiveness allows the lost world to see us suffering like Christ, being betrayed but offering grace to the offender. Again, this in no way excuses or condones the sinful action. And at times, true forgiveness and love means marital separation, removing the addict from the home, police arrest, hospital placement, and intervention.

Defining True Forgiveness

True forgiveness is not forgetting or saying to your spouse that what he or she did (or is doing) is acceptable. True forgiveness is not the cliché saying *forgive and forget*. God knows our sins but chooses to hide our sin with the righteousness of Christ (Colossians 3:2-4). Therefore, we choose to be like God and see our spouses through the lens of Christ's forgiveness—either enslaved to sin in desperate need of the Savior or, if they are believers, hidden in Christ. We offer to them the same grace offered us at Calvary. God's forgiveness is our model and motive. Your forgiveness is not based on your spouse's actions or perceived actions, but on God's grace. From Ken Sande's book, *The Peacemaker*, true forgiveness makes these four promises:

1. I promise I will not dwell on your sin.
2. I promise I will not bring it up or use it against you.
3. I promise I will not talk to others about it.
4. I promise I will not let it stand between us.

The Root of Bitterness and the Cultivator

One of my favorite passages about forgiveness is Hebrews 12:14: "Make every effort to live in peace with all men and to be holy; without holiness no one will see the Lord. See to it that no one misses the grace of God and that no bitter root grows up to cause trouble and defile many." When bitterness grows around our hearts, the tangled roots suffocate us until our hearts grow hard to the work Jesus accomplished for us on the cross. We become controlling and manipulative. We blame our shattered dreams on the "bigger" sinner. We become investigators instead of a good husband or wife, and we slowly drift from the clarity of grace to a fog of judgment.

We must call in the Cultivator! In these times of tremendous hurt, we must focus on the cross as we abide with the Cultivator. He will cut back every branch or root that does not reflect his grace to us. Jesus explains, "I am the true vine, and my Father is the gardener. He cuts off every branch in me that bears no fruit, while every branch that does bear fruit he prunes so that it will be even more fruitful."[24] Allow God to start pruning away the bitter roots that have suffocated your joy. Let him cultivate you a new life of freedom in forgiveness.

Common Pitfalls in Betrayal

This chapter is not big enough to hold all the different types of betrayal. I will, however, briefly explain a couple common pitfalls we can fall prey to when suffering from betrayal. These pitfalls stem from natural desires that can war against our souls in times of betrayal.

The first desire is the craving to pay back your spouse or the person who has sinned against you. It is far too easy to think, *revenge*! Guard your heart from "getting back" at the offender. You will only cause more hurt if you have your own affair or withhold your love or stop sharing your thoughts and emotions.

The second desire involves anxiety over unrealistic boundaries. The boundaries to prevent sin are necessary. Many are necessary, such as Internet filters or not having alcohol in the house. But the boundaries do not define the relationship. Christ defines you and your spouse. You must remain rooted in Christ. He is your identity, not your spouse or another person, or the circumstances of the day.

Often we begin to see ourselves as little holy spirits in the offender's life. In the case of a repentant believer, the Holy Spirit is the guide. You are not your spouse's holy spirit. Boundaries can give you a sense of security and can be helpful. But the ultimate goal is reconciliation and spiritual growth. Boundaries won't be in place forever. After all, God isn't after the pretense of holy living by looking good on the outside. God wants a *heart* that is transformed and yearns for holiness. Allow for opportunities to see growth, so your trust can also begin to grow. A controlling heart offers little opportunity. Now we will examine a few common pitfalls on the road to forgiveness.

Pitfall #1: Abandoned

Being sinned against adds another facet to suffering. Sure you can't control any trials that come to you, but you know they are God ordained. However, when someone sins against you, it is another human that goes *against* your will in a particular situation, often against what is good, holy, or beneficial for you. Your desire is normally for something good, possibly even God-honoring, and he or she betrays your vulnerable trust. You may feel like your dreams and desires are being taken from you. In situations such as physical or sexual abuse, rape, an affair, or living with a spouse, parent, or child who has an addiction—it is easy to believe that God has completely abandoned you. You begin thinking *if God were real He would never have allowed these horrific events or this repeated sin against me.*

In this situation, Scripture is comforting to show us that we are not the only person to experience this type of suffering, God has not and will never abandon us, and though we most likely will never understand why it happened, God is working it to good *somehow* (even if there is no earthly 'good' ever known).

Again, it is good to be reminded that we are part of God's story, and we can't see the whole grand narrative from our vantage point. Second Samuel 13 is a biblical account of innocence stolen by rape and hatred induced-murder that led to the downfall of King David. In all of this suffering, God still brought forth the Messiah. Though the story of Tamar is sobering, it is refreshing to read Scripture and see her referenced as if she were David's only beautiful, noble daughter. The message of 2 Samuel still applies today. It is a call to action, to fight sin and not be silent when you see sin in others. It is a call to repentance, as God's people suffer for past sins. It is also a call to faith, to remember God's grace to redeem his children despite their sins. It displays his provision for people in every age, showing faithfulness to them. It declares the fulfillment of the promised Messiah, Jesus Christ, who is and will be our perfect King. As God showed his sovereignty to bring forth the Messiah through all of Israel's defeats and victories, He is faithfully showing all Christians no matter the circumstance, He is gloriously powerful to bring about his Kingdom.

Pitfall #2: Alone

Another pitfall is to believe that no one can understand the pain you are going through. Perhaps in your circle of friends this adversity is not common. Have you found yourself rolling your eyes when someone shares a trial they are struggling with? Do you diminish people's suffering because your pain seems greater?

God has not asked us to compare our circumstances with another. He has told us his grace is sufficient in our personal weaknesses.

Pitfall #3: Isolated

The enemy uses betrayal to destroy us spiritually in two ways. First, he taunts us with guilt, shame, or hopelessness. We do not share our struggles because people would be disgusted or judge us. Are you so ashamed that you have never shared your pain with anyone, but it burdens you daily with its weight? We can internalize the shame until we have a skewed understanding of our identity. Have you believed you are worthless and have nothing to offer God or the church? The message of the Savior becomes lost in the feelings of abandonment. Isolation sets in. Depression and despair become life's mantra.

The second ploy of the enemy is just as dangerous. Because of the sins done against us we only see that sin, never our own. The bitterness, anger, control, and pride are buried under hurt, focusing on the other person's sins. I do not mean you are to take responsibility for someone's sinful actions against you . . . by no means! They are held accountable for every wrongdoing and poor decision.

But just as Jesus explained in the parable about forgiveness (Matthew 18), we are to forgive as God in Christ forgave us. We all are sinners, but when you have been offended by someone else it is hard to see God's grace in your own sinful life. If you have accepted Jesus as your Savior, He has washed you clean and fights your battles. First Corinthians 6:11 says, "But you were washed, you were sanctified, you were justified in the name of the Lord Jesus Christ and by the Spirit of our God." Don't allow someone else's sin to paralyze you from seeing your own. We are held accountable for our own thoughts, words, and actions. God is after our individual hearts.

Attacking Anxiety

If you have been sinned against seriously, you most likely suffer from anxiety. What I have come to know as the most important method to guard against anxiety is to take your thoughts captive. Second Corinthians 10:3-5 gives us this powerful technique: "demolish arguments and every pretension that sets itself up against the knowledge of God, and take captive every thought to make it obedient to Christ."

Taking anxious thoughts captive helps us focus on truth and rebuilds trust. What does *fighting strongholds* mean practically? Scripture is clear how to do this, but often our thoughts have become comfortable so we do not use this battle plan. According to Corinthians, to fight this battle we must first take captive every hurtful or untrue thought that enters our mind, making it incapable of damage.

In war, captivity deactivates an enemy from being a threat. If you take your thoughts captive and make them obedient to Christ, they will never turn into sinful thoughts, words, or actions. Here is the bottom line: We fight strongholds by destroying any harmful thought before it advances to sin.

When a thought enters your mind that is not true or is blatantly sinful, you are to battle. This means do not dwell on it, fantasize, or analyze the thought. Whether put there by your own flesh or by the enemy, it is a temptation to embrace it. Resist. Do not befriend an enemy of truth. Even if the original thought is true, if it is not edifying, we are told to take it captive.

Second Corinthians calls us to demolish arguments that war against truth by taking them captive *and making them obedient to the gospel*. What has the gospel accomplished in your life? Has it put to death the old man and created you into a new man? If so, do not feed the old dead. Instead interrogate all thoughts in view of your new life covered by the cross.

If the thoughts are against the truth found in Scripture, kill them by putting on truth. In the midst of attack, some practical ways to take thoughts captive and put on truth can be (1) reciting a memorized Scripture pertaining to that struggle, (2) reading the Bible, (3) praying specifically about the attack, (4) calling a friend at the time of attack, and (5) spending time each day with your Savior and Lord, the Commander. Suit up with the armor God gives us through his Word (Ephesians 6).

Martin Luther said, "A bird can land on your head, but you don't have to let it build a nest!" A bad thought may enter your mind, but you don't have to let it dwell there. If you are in Christ, you are a kingdom soldier. Fight with the power of the resurrected Lord. Never Give Up!

Biblical Study and Practical Application

1. If you are dealing with a repentant sinner, then create, type, and sign a contract between all parties affected by the sin. This document should include the four promises of forgiveness mentioned in this chapter.

2. If marital unfaithfulness has occurred (adultery, pornography, emotional affair, etc.) and your spouse is repentant, you can either add to the above contract or create another one that states your covenantal vows of faithfulness to one another. From this day on you commit to

honor one another emotionally, physically, and spiritually as the one-flesh unit God has created you into upon your wedding vows.

3. Saturate yourself in God's Word. Study biblical forgiveness. Read each passage and journal about what God is teaching you personally and to apply it to others. Make notecards of these verses (and others you find) so that you can review them throughout the day. Suggested verses: Psalm 32; Psalm 51; Psalm 103; Micah 6:6-8; Matthew 5:5:38-42; Matthew 6:14-15, 7:1-5; Matthew 18:21-35; Mark 11:20-25; Acts 7:54-60; Romans 12:17-21; Ephesians 4:33-5:2; Colossians 3:12-13; James 4:1-10.

4. When you've been sinned against, it is easy to think the one who has sinned must spend the rest of their lives in your debt. It becomes easy to deny serving him or her. Fight this by planning a special occasion for your loved one. Working to serve this person on a regular basis will create a God-given depth of love. When you don't feel like serving, remember (and memorize) Colossians 3:23-24.

5. Make an action plan to battle sin. See *Appendix D* for an example.

Section Two: Hurting Marriages

Chapter Four

The Divorce Delusion

Jesus said, "Have you not read that he who created them from the beginning made them male and female, and said, 'Therefore a man shall leave his father and his mother and hold fast to his wife, and the two shall become one flesh'? So they are no longer two but one flesh. What therefore God has joined together, let not man separate."
Matthew 19:4-6

'Til death do us part. On my wedding day, I will not be saying that sentence. Not that I'm not in it to win it -- I am -- only that if two people are told they can never leave, how do they know the other really wants to stay? Marriage is hard enough without the specter of death being the only way out hanging over our heads. To me, it's just another fire and brimstone tactic absentmindedly handed down from generation to generation just to get people to stay in line. Or give them comfort that once they kiss, they will always be there for each other. And in a country with a healthy divorce rate and prenuptial agreements -- which are essentially Plan Bs before the ink on Plan A is even dry -- I think it's safe to assume there are a lot of examples of things not working out to pay attention to. This is one of

the areas where the evangelical church needs to grow most -- learning how to minister to a society that can no longer be scared straight. The church has to figure out a way to talk about relationships and marriage the way it is framed today, without all of the threats. Or risk being left behind.

- CNN Journalist, LZ Granderson

The Challenge

Marriage doomsayer and covenantal vow-keeper alike can see that divorce is abundantly evasive in our world today. Therefore, the need to rediscover the biblical view is critical. If Christians, who live their lives according to Scripture, do not heed this call to action—by not only teaching truth, but also personally living it out—Granderson is right. The church will suffer. The issue of marriage already is and will be the major debate for evangelical Christianity in the coming decades.

If you search the Internet for any length of time, you will find site after site affirming a new definition of marriage and encouragement to divorce for the sake of personal happiness. Tragically most Christians have studied little what Scripture says on this topic. I state that with a confident assessment from my own personal counseling experiences. In almost every conversation I've had on this topic with a struggling married person, a friend, or a family member the response was, "but doesn't God allow divorce if someone's unhappy?" Or as the court system defines irreconcilable differences.

When we studied what the Bible actually stated on this topic, they were shocked. In every case, this newfound truth gave them biblical insight and a passion to fight for their marriages and hope for restoration! Counselor Jay Adams appropriately conveys the *concept of divorce* as biblical. Therefore, he instructs Christians to do all they can to understand it and to teach what God, and his Word, say about it.[25] Adams states, unlike marriage, divorce is a human institution, for God in his perfection designed marriage to be permanent.[26]

One of the greatest passions my husband and I share is to teach biblical marriage, so men and women can flourish in their relationships as they join together for an adventure guided by the Lord, Jesus Christ. Honestly, I'm quite certain this marriage and divorce topic elevates my blood pressure, as my head and heart explode with the plea to "do it God's way!" As with everything in life, when humanity tries to invent a "better" way of living life rather than God's best, it ends in brokenness. Remember the Garden of Eden? Same temptation, same result! Anytime we try to fulfill our desires of pleasure, control, happiness, and love in ways detached from the Creator, it results in suffering. Momentary gratification or happiness does not constitute successful living.

In Chapter One we discussed the reason God commands us to live according to his Word is for our own good . . . our best, his Glory. Christianity is not a religion of wooden rituals and rules but rather a call to God's joy! The problem is too many Christians disbelieve God loves them and does what is best for them. They look miserable as they try to fulfill their desires in their own ways.

The Divorce Epidemic

"Church attendance has not been declining since the 1970s because people are shacking up. It's because the church as a whole has become stagnant while the society it's based in continues to evolve," CNN Journalist Granderson claims. "Couple that with the disconnect between how we're told to live our lives and the lives being led by those doing the telling, and you can see why we're just less religious as a country." Nobody wants to be told to do something by a Pharisee. But when atheists' state among the top reasons not to believe in Jesus is the Christian divorce rate, my heart breaks! Christian, with our individual purpose and our purpose in marriage to share the good news of Jesus Christ to a lost world,[27] this should break your heart as well. Change is needed . . . and fast!

The Barna Research Group's national study claims many evangelical Christians are choosing divorce. Their research shows the divorce rate as 25% for the general population. The Christian divorce rate was 27% compared to 21% for atheists.[28] However, in this study many variables were not discussed, such as cohabitation, pre-marital counseling, church involvement, actual born-again Christian (not just claiming "Christianity" or a denomination), and previous marriages.

As encouragement, Dr. Tom Ellis, former chairman of the Southern Baptist Convention's Council on the Family said that "born-again Christian couples who marry . . . in the church after having received premarital counseling . . . and attend church regularly and pray daily together . . ." experience only one divorce out of nearly 39,000 marriages, or 0.00256 percent!

So, which is it? Honestly, I think these statistics tell us only one thing that matters: Regardless of 27% or .0025%, if the Christian divorce rate is being used by the unbeliever as a reason to deny the existence of God, then something has gone terribly wrong.

We need a renewed perspective and a revived passion of what is most biblical when we define marriage. Theologian Wayne Grudem explains, "The union between husband and wife is not temporary but lifelong, and it is not trivial but is a profound relationship created by God in order to picture the relationship between Christ and his church."[29]

Author of *Sacred Marriage*, Gary Thomas, agrees that Christians need to think of their marriage as a chance to serve Christ: "A Christian who gets divorced puts their happiness before their devotion to Christ." Certainly, there are tragic events—such as unrepentant physical abuse, adultery, and addiction that complicate the marital vows. But for this chapter, we will discuss that divorce is not a biblical option when "unhappily married," which is the delusion many Christians have believed. This choice leads neither to a happy-ever-after divorce nor glorifies God.

Some people may feel relieved after divorcing a burdensome spouse, but neither party leaves the marriage unscathed. Even atheists who have gone through divorce will admit to the brokenness and the horror that accompanies a "happy" or "necessary" divorce. A *New York Times* journalist shares after her affair-induced divorce, "I look at my parents and at how much simpler their lives are at the ages of 75, mostly because they haven't marred the landscape with grand-scale deceit. They have this marriage of 50-some years behind them, and it is a monument to success. A few weeks or months of illicit passion could not hold a candle to it."[30]

Defining Marriage

God designed the marriage union prior to the fall. The marital institution was based upon a "one-flesh" union, between one man and one woman, in complete faithfulness, only to be severed with death.[31]

Old Testament Covenantal Vow

Marriage is a covenant.[32] It is defined as a sacred bond between a man and a woman established by and publicly entered into before God, as "an agreement that a faithful person would not break even if the partner to whom that person is in covenant breaks the stipulations of the covenant."[33] While there are various types of covenants established in Old Testament, the term "covenant" in general conveys "the idea of a solemn commitment, guaranteeing promises or obligations undertaken by one or both parties."[34]

Even in the Old Testament law, salvation was found only in God, based on him fulfilling the covenant, not the people's obedience. In short, God makes the rules, not us. And it's God's commitment that makes a covenant important. God is the one sustaining a covenant. God says in Leviticus, "You reject My statutes, and if your soul abhors My ordinances so as not to carry out all My commandments, and so break My covenant . . . [I will punish you] . . .Yet in spite of this, when they are in the land of their enemies, I will not reject them...nor break My covenant with them; for I am the Lord their God."[35] Again God cries, "I will *never* break My covenant with you."[36] Both the old and new covenants are founded upon God's unconditional love. Salvation in the Old Testament was no more dependent on human's obedience, than in the New Testament—though a perfect sacrifice was required.

Professor and author, Dr. Daniel Heimbach explains that the marriage covenant is a relationship between three parties: God, a husband, and a wife. A covenant is not primarily a legal bond, but is a spiritual and moral bond. And God holds us accountable for our spiritual covenants.[37]

New Testament Covenantal Vow

Marriage is rooted in creation and the will of the Creator himself. As D.A. Carson emphasizes, "If marriage is grounded in creation, in the way God has made us, it cannot be reduced to a merely [human] covenant relationship that breaks down when the covenantal promises are broken."[38] When God instituted marriage at creation, divorce was not permitted. For a husband or a wife to divorce a spouse means to act against the will of the Creator for marriage.

In the New Covenant, this "holy nation" and "royal priesthood" found in 1 Peter 2:9 is given a more challenging standard than ever before. Salvation continues to be 100% the generous gift of God through the perfect sacrifice of Christ, but Jesus calls his followers to fulfill a new standard of love that displays his power working within them: To deny the pursuit of happiness on selfish terms and to deny their attempts to fulfill their own personal desires.

The marriage covenant is one of the most beautiful reflections of God's unconditional covenant with his people—and a perfect opportunity to deny selfish pursuits! The New Covenant established by Christ with his church is a permanent relationship created by a redemptive act of love. This act of love—

when Christ gave himself on the cross—cleanses the church so He might present her to himself as glorious. It's not just your happiness that is at stake with your marriage; it's also the great romance Christ has with his bride, the church.

Understanding Divorce in Scripture

As discussed earlier in this chapter, divorce in American culture is not only practiced, but also pursued as a simple solution to marital woes. I fully acknowledge that after decades of research on this topic by some of the finest Christian scholars, the conclusion to this sensitive topic is still heavily debated. The purpose of this book is not to debate at great length the exceptions for divorce.[39] My goal is to address the overwhelming amount of marriages that end without biblical justification. And even in cases of adultery and abandonment, the power of Christ is capable to restore a broken marriage. God can redeem anyone! In the remaining part of this chapter we are going to explore what Scripture says about divorce to understand God's best for us.

Sin and Reconciliation

When sin is hurting a marriage, it is clear God's greatest desire is reconciliation with your spouse, no matter the offense. Reconciliation, the forgiveness and restoration of a husband's and wife's fellowship, is a beautiful work of God. Just like the sinner brought to forgiveness in Jesus, God can use a broken marriage union to joyfully proclaim the sacrificial love of Christ for his bride, the church.

As we discuss divorce, we are addressing a sin issue from one or both spouses. (If you are the spouse abandoned or the victim of an affair, please understand as previously mentioned you are not responsible for your spouse's sin). Selfishness to pursue our desires is the leading cause of divorce. Sure, we may call it adultery, addiction, abuse, anger, or any number of things, but self-worship is the root of the matter.

The opposite of self-worship is God-worship. Having a life defined by love is what Jesus told the disciples would be a mark of the true believer. The true believer loves other people and obeys God's commandments. Jesus explained, this is "spoken to you, that [my] joy may be in you, and that your joy may be full" (John 15:10-11). So as in all of life—including marriage—we also must get a renewed perspective and a revived passion that God is after our ultimate Joy!

Divorce Logic from Scripture

It is clear from Scripture that the marriage unit is one established by God, covenanted for life, and an opportunity to share the gospel. So in our discussion on divorce, we are going to look at what Jesus uses as one of the "worst-case scenarios"—adultery. A key passage is found in Matthew 5, which is part of *The Sermon on the Mount* (found in Matthew 5-7). Enormous crowds followed Jesus to the mountainside where he began teaching them about what being a follower of God really meant.

He starts with the beatitudes that teach how to be blessed in this life, contrary to how the world may define blessing and success. He addresses the call for believers to be the "salt and light" of the world. Jesus reveals how He has come not to abolish the Law, but to fulfill the Law of the Old Testament. Then Jesus gets specific: anger, lust, divorce, vows, revenge, loving enemies, giving to the poor, prayer, fasting, money, worry, judgment, and heaven. We will focus on Jesus' teaching concerning lust, divorce, vows, and forgiveness.

Jesus on Lust

Jesus says in Matthew 5:28 that although the Law has defined adultery to be the sexual act between someone other than your spouse, "I tell you that anyone who looks at a woman lustfully has already committed adultery with her in his heart." The penalty for adultery in Jewish custom was being stoned to death. Lust, especially in the form of pornography, is an epidemic today. There aren't many men or women standing that can say they have never "committed adultery in their hearts." Therefore, does Jesus mean everyone should be stoned for lust? Or is it grounds for divorce?

Jesus on Divorce

In Jesus' teaching on divorce in Matthew 5, let's get some perspective on the cultural scene. The Pharisee's question that arises here is over the permissibility of divorce, "Is it lawful for a man to divorce his wife *for any and every reason*?" (Matthew 19:3). This question is initiated from Deuteronomy 24:1-4, because of a major debate between the two schools of Rabbinic thought—the Shammai and Hillel Schools.

The Pharisees were trying to trap Jesus. The question the Pharisees posed to Jesus (Matthew 19:4) centered on the significance of the phrase "some indecency" found in Deuteronomy 24:1. The Mishna, which contains the oral traditions of Judaism, tells us how the conservative school of Shammai and the liberal school of Hillel interpreted this phrase: "The school of Shammai said: A man may not divorce his wife unless he has discovered something unchaste about her, for it is written, 'Because he has found some unseemly thing in her' (Deuteronomy 24:1). But the school of Hillel said: He may divorce her even if she spoiled a dish for him for it is written, 'Because he has found some unseemly thing in her.'"[40]

It is essential to distinguish that, unlike the Pharisees, Jesus does not restrict his discussion of divorce to Deuteronomy 24. He does not consider it the basic or definitive Old Testament passage on the subject—it was merely a regulation that had to do with a particular sort of problem relating to marriage. Jesus returns to Genesis 2 for his definitive passage—the created order—a man and a woman united as "one person" (one flesh) for life. This, Jesus told them in his answer to their question, is the way marriage is intended to be.

Divorce violates not only God's original plan for marriage, but also the sacred marriage covenant to which the Lord himself is a witness. Divorce is—at its core—a betrayal of humanity's most intimate relationship, a betrayal affecting the very well-being of God's community in the church.

Logically, if Jesus simply agreed with either the school of Hillel or the school of Shammai, the disciples in Matthew 19 would not have been so surprised. Especially if Jesus agreed a spouse can divorce for adultery when Jesus said, "I tell you that anyone who divorces his wife, *except for marital unfaithfulness* and marries another woman commits adultery" (Matthew 19:9; cf. Matthew 5:32). If God created marriage to be indissoluble at creation, what did Jesus mean with this exception? I have two thoughts and a few unanswered questions.

First, the disciples were amazed at this "exception" saying, "If this is the situation between a husband and wife, it is better not to marry" (acknowledging Hebrews 13 if unmarried, chaste). Jesus answers with a "Ya, no kidding! Marriage is hard and permanent. That is why marriage is a gift from God and only to be entered into by those whom it is given."

Perhaps the exception had more to do with the

cultural practice of bethrothal. Remember when Mary and Joseph were bethrothed, before consummating their marriage, Joseph was going to *divorce* Mary quietly when she was found pregnant with Jesus (Matthew 1:19)? Joseph thought she acted unfaithfully to him. Before the year of bethrothal was fulfilled he had every right to end their engagement.

The majority of scholars believe that Jesus was talking about an actual physical act of sexual sin. It is possible He permitted divorce in this case, since this form of betrayal is terrible. However, if this is what Jesus meant, He was simply agreeing with the school of Shammai.

Second, throughout Scripture, God uses marital unfaithfulness—adultery—as a way to describe Israel's spiritual unfaithfulness, yet he does not divorce them. As representatives of Christ, why would Christians receive a special privilege of divorce for the same act of unfaithfulness? Is sexual sin (i.e. pornography and adultery) the worst and only divorceable sin?

I raise these questions to show how breaking the marriage covenant leads to horrible complications. There are many scholarly and theological explanations for the exception of adultery. However, the scope of this work does not permit me to go through each one. As we study *The Sermon on the Mount*, my hope is to see that *in Christ*, Christians are able to offer forgiveness graciously, experience restoration, and allow vengeance to be enacted by God alone for injustice. Jesus was willing to pay the ultimate sacrifice for his church. You should be willing to go to great lengths to save your marriage. It's worth the effort no matter what you've done or had done to you!

Jesus on Vows

After a discussion on divorce, Jesus continues the Sermon of the Mount with vows. This section of the sermon is fitting since vows precede divorce, and we are often in need of a walk down memory lane when blinded by a present calamity.

On my wedding day, Dustin and I looked deep into each other's eyes and promised our faithful love to the other, "For better or worse, for richer, for poorer, in sickness and in health, to love and to cherish; from this day forward until death do us part." Vows according to Jesus are not to be broken under any circumstance, because they are made to the Lord (Matthew 5:33).

Jesus on Revenge and Forgiveness

The remainder of Matthew 5 is Jesus' call to Christians to deny their own rights, offering forgiveness like God offers to us. Jesus explained, "Love your enemies and pray for those who persecute you that you may be sons of your Father in Heaven . . . If you love those who love you, what reward will you get? Are not even the tax collectors doing that? . . . Be perfect therefore, as your heavenly Father is perfect. If you forgive men when they sin against you, your heavenly

Father will also forgive you. But if you do not forgive men for their sins, your Father will not forgive your sins" (Matthew 5:43-48; 6:14).

Wow! Perfection? Complete forgiveness?

That is why Christ's power is a necessity for loving an unlovable spouse. Anyone can stay in a bad marriage, at least in the sense that you are physically present and under the same roof. But, that's not marriage. Jesus is telling Christians that in order to love in a way that mirrors his grace, a couple must build their house on the solid foundation that will never fall— Jesus, the Perfector of love and forgiveness. Only then can a floundering marriage be made to flourish.

Christian Couple's Call to Action

Reconciliation should always be the initial hope of any marital conflict. Biblical scholar Andreas Köstenberger writes, "Divorce is never willed by God and is always the result of sin. Marital reconciliation in the restoration and preservation of marriage always ought to be the goal and prayer of the individuals concerned."[41] Paul said regarding a person's marital status, "each one should retain the place in life that the Lord assigned to him and to which God has called him" (1 Corinthians 7:17).

Theologian John Murray beautifully sums it up: "The marital institution is sanctified by the forces of redemptive grace to such an extent that it is made one of the main channels for the accomplishment of God's saving purposes in the world. It is in the bosom of the Christian family that the nurture which the Lord himself provides is administered."[42] At creation God had great plans to use marriage as a beacon for his covenant love. His plans have not changed. Let us spur one another on to pursue marriages that blossom with the beauty of the gospel.

Something to Sing About

Don and Julia's marriage was finished. Don was addicted to alcohol. He squandered all their money and become a delinquent father and husband. Julia couldn't stay around any longer. She moved out with the kids. He was hurting himself, her, and especially their young children. Julia even had begun talking to other men for comfort. After some persuasion by a friend, Don admitted himself into an addictions ministry. Julia believed her decision to divorce Don was justified. She knew God wanted her to be happy and have a better marriage. As a last effort, she also sought out some counseling. One session, Julia learned about true biblical marriage: the joy, the pain, the battle, and the victories. She cried tired, hopeful tears that day.

Soon Don and Julia were in counseling together. They began to understand what a covenant in marriage means, and they both promised to fight for their marriage. They began having hope that God could restore their wrecked marriage, making it into something that flourished. Months went by and progress was slow, but soon Don and Julia began truly living their hopes of a good marriage. They moved back home together. Never before had they been vulnerable, fought sin, and seriously run after the Lord together. Years have now passed and a new baby was added to their family. Trials still come and trust continues to grow. Redemption is a daily reminder to Julia when she looks at her children and husband. How different life would have been had she given this all up just for the sake of her personal happiness. The choice to follow God's way brought true joy and fulfillment. Julia wholeheartedly believes, "If our marriage—what was left of it—could be made new, don't give up. In the power of Christ, yours can too!"

God uses even a difficult marriage for our good. It becomes one method God uses to sanctify us and bring us near. Remember, God desires his children to be made into the likeness of Christ. He wants to grow you through the struggles and blessings of marriage. God can make your marriage into something to sing about. One day you will shout with the psalmist, "For you, O Lord, have made me glad by your work; at the works of your hands I sing for joy" (Psalm 92:4).

Biblical Application and Practical Study

1. Personally study marriage and divorce in Scripture. Journal (1) what the Lord is teaching you, (2) what lies you have believed about marriage and divorce from culture, (3) how God

wants you to respond. Here are some passages to study: Genesis 2; Malachi 2:14-16; Proverbs 2:16-17; Matthew 5; Matthew 19; Mark 10:6-10; Luke 16:18; Ephesians 5:23-32; 1 Corinthians 7:11; and Hebrews 13).

2. Complete a study on the attributes of God (suggestion: Paul David Washer, *The One True God*). When studying the characteristics of God, connect how a Christ-follower is supposed to act by loving others.

3. Carefully answer this question: Are you doing a good job of being Christ to an unlovable spouse? Write it out in paragraph form.

4. Read *When Sinners Say I Do* by Dave Harvey and discuss each chapter as a couple.

5. Complete this forgiveness activity with your spouse: Make a list of all the sins you have committed against your spouse and all the sins your spouse has committed against you. Exchange lists and add anything forgotten. Read Matthew 5:43-48 and Matthew 18 together. Go outside and burn the lists. Then pray together.

CHAPTER FIVE

MARITAL MAYHEM

Whoever would be great among you must be your servant, and whoever would be first among you must be slave of all. For even the Son of Man came not to be served but to serve, and to give his life as a ransom for many."
Mark 10:43-45.

If you've been married for longer than a week, then you know that every day of marriage isn't a "bed of roses." Life happens. Emotions go up—and down. Sin strikes. And trials take the joy right out of "happily ever after." Nonetheless, God intended marriage to be a joy. Marriage is a gift! God said, "He who finds a wife finds what is good and receives favor from the Lord" (Proverbs 18:22).

Joy should be the mark of the Christian. Joy in marriage is no exception. From personal experience I can say that marriage can be the most fulfilling, passion-filled, happiest relationship on earth! If you agree with God's Word that marriage is a lifelong covenant and a fertile ground for gracious forgiveness, then understand that it is also one of the main relationships Satan will try to destroy.

First Peter explains, "Do not be surprised at the fiery ordeal that has come on you to test you, as though something strange were happening to you. But rejoice inasmuch as you participate in the sufferings of Christ, so that you may be overjoyed when his glory is revealed."[43] Sometimes marriage can be a fiery ordeal, and Satan will use the trial to break the covenant bond between husband and wife.

A Christ-Centered Marriage

As mentioned in the previous chapter, our purpose in marriage is to mirror God's image. After God created the earth and the animals, He said, "Let Us make man in Our image, according to Our likeness; and let them rule over the fish of the sea and over the birds of the sky and over the cattle and over all the earth, and over every creeping thing that creeps on the earth." The account continues, "God created man in his own image, in the image of God He created him; male and female He created them." Starting with creation we can see God's plan for marriage unfold with the first couple—Adam and Eve. God's first purpose for creating man and woman and joining them in marriage was to mirror his image on earth.

The Hebrew word for "mirror" means to reflect God, to magnify, exalt, and glorify him. Your marriage should reflect God's image to a world that desperately needs to see who He is. Since we're created in the image of God, people who wouldn't otherwise know

God, should be able to look at us and get a glimpse, especially as we fulfill the roles God has given us as man and woman.

Foundational Principles

Counselor and Professor, Dr. Robert Jones, gives three foundational principles for marriage:

1. God created and established marriage.
2. God ordained marriage as a covenant relationship, under him, with your spouse. God gives marriage as a covenant for life; this covenant should not be broken.
3. God regulates marriage by revealing his counsel in Scripture about how marriages should be established and lived out.

According to Genesis, God had a perfect plan for the husband and wife, more specially, a plan for humanity. However, the fall of humanity in Genesis 3 caused sin to enter the world, which distorted the roles for husbands and wives. Nonetheless, God created and still regulates marriage to be between one man and one woman for life.

These very foundations are being challenged in our world as we see God's regulations rejected for the lusts of the flesh: pornography, divorce, affairs, homosexuality, and co-habitation. These are issues we must be prepared to give a biblical answer for because they are the heavily debated topics of our generation, even within our churches (1 Peter 3:15). Anything different from God's perfect design at creation cannot offer complete fulfillment or mirror the image of God.

What Is a Christian Marriage and Why Is it Different?

A Christian marriage is a union between two sinners who find forgiveness for their sins in Jesus Christ and who seek to extend that forgiveness to each other. They make progress in overcoming their sins, and becoming and doing more of what God wants them to be. My husband and I stole our martial identity from Gary Thomas in *Sacred* Marriage, who coined the term, *couple-saint*. We're two different people joined together in one flesh, helping each other get to "well done good and faithful servant."

Getting Practical: Roles, Communication, and Conflict

It is easy to get discouraged or feel discontent in marriage. Questions plague us: *Did I marry the right person? Why doesn't he understand me? If she would just do what I ask? This is not the happily-ever-after I imagined?* And on they go . . .

God created us in the real world. Along came sin. We have real problems and real life to work through. We know our spouses and marriages are not perfect. It is God's grace that makes *your* spouse *your* "soul-mate!" And it is God's grace that makes marriage worth pursuing for a lifetime. So, let's get practical and discuss biblical roles, communication, and conflict.

What Is My Role?

I know. I know. Women, you're thinking, "If she says 'submit' to my gorilla of a husband, I'm closing this book and never opening it again!" And men, you're thinking, "She better say, 'my wife is to respect and submit to me,' cause this woman is impossible!"

A discussion on roles is about as controversial as you can get in a marital counseling case. But the Creator once again lays a beautiful foundation to display his image through the marital unit that gives joy, as husband and wife fulfill their roles.

First, we will discuss the husbands. As head of the household your role sets the overall attitude for a wife fulfilling her role. Most significantly, you will be held accountable for how you lead your family.

Husbands (Ephesians 5:25-30)

Husband, love your wife as Christ sacrificially gave of his entire life for his bride, the church. Sacrificial love is the mark of the role-fulfilling husband. Early church father John Chrysostom writes, "Hear the measure of love. Would you want that your wife should obey you as the Church does Christ? Have care for her, as Christ for the Church; and if it should be needful that you should give your life for her, or be cut to pieces a thousand times, or endure anything whatever, refuse it not; yea, if you have suffered this you have not done what Christ did, for you do this for one to whom you are already united, but He for who rejected Him and hated Him" (St. John Chrysostom in Abbott, ICC Comm. On Ephesians 5:25, contemporized by Dr. Robert D. Jones).

That is true love. Scripture even gives practical ways to love your wife sacrificially: read Scripture over her to encourage her, challenge her, and comfort her soul. Think of her desires as more important than your own. Guard her heart with faithful, tender care. Protect her body and heart as if it were your own. Be kind, not harsh. Build her up through admonishing words. Fight for your marriage. Pursue her in a way she feels most adored. Fulfill her sexual desires. Forgive all sins committed against you. Show sensitivity as you listen to her fears, concerns, and joys. Grow trust by faithful living. Nourish her, cherish her, and if the situation arose, give your life to protect her.

According to 1 Peter, husbands must lead and care for their wives in a way that protects her spirit, heart, and body so that your prayers—your relationship with Christ—are not hindered. Lead your wife by providing wise, godly direction for her and your entire family. Remember, true leadership is service-oriented like Christ, a servant leader.

Wives (Ephesians 5:22-24)

The truth is many of us desire to be the "top

dog." Taking orders from others, especially against our own *better* ideas or desires, is difficult. And if suffering isn't your s-word, perhaps submission is. That simple 6-letter word—S-U-B-M-I-T—can have quite the bitter taste. Satan whispers: "humility is demeaning" or "service is slavery."

Being a "door-mat" or victim of abuse by domination is not at the heart of Paul, Peter, John, or Jesus. Submission does not mean you should just accept being the victim of violence. According to Scripture, submitting can be the most God-like we could ever become, both for men and women. Ephesians says, "Follow God's example, therefore, as dearly loved children and walk in the way of love, just as Christ loved us and *gave himself up for us* as a fragrant offering and sacrifice to God" (Ephesians 5:1-2).

In the ultimate act of love, Jesus Christ relinquished his own desires to be with the Father in paradise. By dying for our sin, He broke perfect fellowship with God! God the Son spoke to God the Father, "Not my will, but yours, be done." For Jesus, the greatest act of submission possible caused him the severest of pain that resulted in glorious joy. This is the beauty of godly submission in marriage: *Not my will, but yours, be done.*

A helpful definition for submission comes from Dr. Robert Jones, who explains submission is *to place yourself willingly under the authority and direction of the person whom God has placed as a leader over you.* Therefore, as a wife, your role in submission is to discern and *do* what your husband *desires* you to do, to please Jesus Christ, unless it violates your conscious.

Biblical submission involves the heart and includes a wife's attitude, not merely her actions. This is why Paul says for women to "urge the younger women to love their husbands and children, to be self-controlled and pure, to be busy at home, to be kind, and to be subject to their husbands, so that no one will malign the word of God" (Titus 2:4-5). Submission carries the weight of love, respect, duties, provision, and godliness. Submission is the fruit of the spirit in one word. After the fruit of the spirit are listed out, Scripture declares, "Those who belong to Christ Jesus have crucified the flesh with its passions and desires."

If Jesus was called to submit, as his followers would we not expect the same call? Wives, Jesus commands you to submit to your husband in everything, except sinful things. If your husband is not a good communicator, seek out his desires and speak with him about them. Do not be silent waiting for his leadership. You are his God-given helper. Help him fulfill his role of leadership! Be the one your husband feels most confident delegating to. Scripture explains that the freedom and joy of submission, even when your husband may not be leading well, is to do it to please Jesus. Jesus is worthy of your submission!

Why Fulfilling Your Role is So Difficult

After defining our roles biblically, it sounds so

easy: Love and submit to your compassionate, servant-leader husband who desires to please Jesus at all times. Sure! Maybe in a perfect world! Where did it go wrong? We go all the way back to the beginning. In Genesis 3:1-24, we read the account of the fall. God only gave one forbiddance: The Tree of Good and Evil. Everything else was to be enjoyed. In God's beautiful care for his new creatures, He was protecting them from knowing both good *and* evil. He desired their good, every moment, and forever.

Enter Satan. Like a Shakespearean tragedy, the reader's heart quickens as the evil antagonist comes on to the scene—fearing this will not end well. Have you ever wondered why Satan targeted Eve, not Adam. James 3 explains, "Whoever is wise will show it by their deeds done in humility. But whoever harbors bitter envy and selfish ambition, such wisdom does not come from heaven, but is unspiritual, demonic. There you find disorder and every evil practice. But the wisdom that comes from heaven is first of all pure; then peace-loving, considerate, submissive, full of mercy and good fruit, impartial and sincere."[44]

Submission and humility are the opposite of demonic ambitions. Satan did not like his God-given role as a servant so he targeted the helper/submissive role first (i.e. Eve). Satan had to know since this method of stealing God's glory had not worked for him, it also would not work for her. He succeeded in awarding her the same fate he received: broken fellowship with God and man.

He's been distorting roles ever since.

Eve led the way into sin. Adam allowed the deception of his wife, abandoning his role as head. Eve was deceived. Adam passively stood by and willingly ate. Satan struck at their roles. He usurped Adam's headship and fed Eve the bait, "Wouldn't you rather be in charge, Eve?"

Part of the curse given to women is "Your desire will be for your husband, and he will rule over you" (Genesis 3:16). Or "You will desire to control your husband, but he will rule over you" (NLT).

Husbands and wives would now have ongoing conflict. In contrast to the ideal conditions in the Garden of Eden and the harmony between Adam and Eve, their relationship from that point on would include a power struggle. Eve would desire to rule over her husband, but her husband would instead rule over her.

At the root of sin is disunity—both with God and others. The battle of the sexes had begun. Both man and woman would now seek the upper hand in marriage. The man who was to lovingly care for and nurture his wife would now seek to rule her through dominance, and the wife would desire to take control from her husband. Sin birthed disunity.

As with all sin, we must battle our natural, sinful desires to fight for God's best. In this case, God's best is a loving, gentle, and servant-leader husband who leads his respectful, submissive wife to honor God with every moment and every decision in life. Praise the Lord, we aren't left simply to embrace the curse or try our hardest to fulfill our roles.

Genesis 3:15 tells us the Seed of the woman would crush Satan's head! Christ would come through a woman—Mary—and defeat evil. Therefore, God not only offers us salvation for our eternal souls, He gives us the power because of Christ's work to live for him. Now, because of this work of Christ dying and living for us, we have opportunity to display the relationship of Christ and the church in our marriages.

Anybody There? The Necessity of Communication and Vulnerability

Several studies point to the fact that women use more words than men in any given day. The disparity of only 1500 words! It seems this statistic is revealed as an epiphany to understanding the opposite sex. For some, whether a man or woman, communication can be difficult. Nonetheless, we are told "if possible, so far as it depends on [us], live peaceably with all" (Romans 12:18). And to attain peace we must pour our lives in our relationships—which requires communication. And we must do so without corrupt talk coming from our mouths—which requires *good* communication.

Out of the Mouth Speaks the Heart

The Bible explains that like a tree, a person is

known by their fruit, whether good or bad, useful or useless: "The good person out of the good treasure of his heart produces good, and the evil person out of his evil treasure produces evil, for out of the abundance of the heart his mouth speaks."[45] If we're honest, we will agree that we speak exactly what we believe, what we want to say, and how we want to say it! Blame it on being hungry and cranky (that's my confession), what is in our hearts comes out. A selfish heart breeds sinful communication.

Psalms gives the formula to guard us from our "word vomit." We should "seek the Lord with all our hearts" and "hide his Word in our hearts" so that we do not sin against God or others (Psalm 119:10-11). The fundamentals of good communication do not start with words at all. They start with listening well. In my marriage there are times I unload a distressing situation on my husband...sparing no detail! Sometimes during my rant, my Mr. Handyman husband wants to give me advice to my problems and...fix-it! Though his advice is normally exactly what I need to hear, he has learned that all I want in those moments is for him to listen first.

A couple practical ways to grasp Christ-like listening are to (1) Listen actively and attentively, and (2) Listen caringly and compassionately. God gave us communication as a gift and it goes two-ways. Listen and speak. (This is also a good practice in prayer . . . we often forget to listen).

After listening, then we speak godly encouragement and advice. From *Peacemakers*, Ken

Sande gives four qualities of godly speech based on Ephesians 4:25-5:2 and a helpful acronym: (1) Honest (4:25)—Tell the whole truth, be vulnerable. (2) Beneficial (4:29)—Attack problems, not people. (3) Timely (4:29)—Keep current, don't bring up forgiven past garbage, and (4) Kindly (4:31-5:2)—Act, don't react. Ask yourself when communicating to THINK.

THINK
T - Is it true?
H - Is it helpful?
I - Is it inspiring?
N - Is it necessary?
K - Is it kind?

When we communicate, "May the words of our mouth and the meditation of our hearts be pleasing in your sight, O LORD, my Rock and my Redeemer" (Psalm 19:14). We must view our marital communication as ministry to our spouse.

Conflict

Conflict in marriage is inevitable. It will happen, so expect it. Conflicts are most often sinful and must be resolved. View them as opportunities to learn from and grow together in your relationship. In fact, conflict is a great opportunity to be gospel people. Practice ministering actions to your spouse by serving with a thankful, loving heart and do nothing out of selfish ambition. If your spouse is hostile or unloving, then provide for him or her, expecting nothing in return. Make pleasing God your single and all-consuming concern.

Accountability and Vulnerable Intimacy

Every night before bed, my husband and I share the day's events, temptations, our failures, and godly victories. We offer one another biblical truth, practical advice, and encouragement to continue battling in this thing called life. Develop good communication and vulnerable accountability with your spouse. It produces trust, spurs on a deeper relationship with God and one another, and makes dreams come true as you share together in daily routines.

Pursue

I'm a planner, but I love surprises! Whether you enjoy planning surprises, date nights, or random gifts for your spouse—fight the desire to take a back seat to your marriage. Christ pursues his bride. He teaches her, listens to her, and plans the most amazing blessings (even through trials and suffering). We should mirror God in every way. Don't neglect pursuing your spouse. Even if you aren't good at creative surprises or the plans flop, remember the old adage: It's the thought that counts! Keep the passion alive and pursue your spouse.

Sande gives four qualities of godly speech based on Ephesians 4:25-5:2 and a helpful acronym: (1) Honest (4:25)—Tell the whole truth, be vulnerable. (2) Beneficial (4:29)—Attack problems, not people. (3) Timely (4:29)—Keep current, don't bring up forgiven past garbage, and (4) Kindly (4:31-5:2)—Act, don't react. Ask yourself when communicating to THINK.

> THINK
> T - Is it true?
> H - Is it helpful?
> I - Is it inspiring?
> N - Is it necessary?
> K - Is it kind?

When we communicate, "May the words of our mouth and the meditation of our hearts be pleasing in your sight, O LORD, my Rock and my Redeemer" (Psalm 19:14). We must view our marital communication as ministry to our spouse.

Conflict

Conflict in marriage is inevitable. It will happen, so expect it. Conflicts are most often sinful and must be resolved. View them as opportunities to learn from and grow together in your relationship. In fact, conflict is a great opportunity to be gospel people. Practice ministering actions to your spouse by serving with a thankful, loving heart and do nothing out of selfish ambition. If your spouse is hostile or unloving, then provide for him or her, expecting nothing in return. Make pleasing God your single and all-consuming concern.

Accountability and Vulnerable Intimacy

Every night before bed, my husband and I share the day's events, temptations, our failures, and godly victories. We offer one another biblical truth, practical advice, and encouragement to continue battling in this thing called life. Develop good communication and vulnerable accountability with your spouse. It produces trust, spurs on a deeper relationship with God and one another, and makes dreams come true as you share together in daily routines.

Pursue

I'm a planner, but I love surprises! Whether you enjoy planning surprises, date nights, or random gifts for your spouse—fight the desire to take a back seat to your marriage. Christ pursues his bride. He teaches her, listens to her, and plans the most amazing blessings (even through trials and suffering). We should mirror God in every way. Don't neglect pursuing your spouse. Even if you aren't good at creative surprises or the plans flop, remember the old adage: It's the thought that counts! Keep the passion alive and pursue your spouse.

The Gift of Marriage

Marriage should be a joyful union. You and your spouse get to share life's adventures together. I hope you grow to experience a thriving marriage. It is a beautiful, fulfilling gift from the Lord. We will end this chapter with the early church father, Tertullian. He writes beautiful words about marriage: "How beautiful, then, the marriage of two Christians, two who are one in hope, one in desire, one in the way of life they follow, one in the religion they practice. They are as brother and sister, both servants of the same Master. Nothing divides them, either in flesh or in spirit. They pray together, they worship together, they fast together; instructing one another, encouraging one another, strengthening one another. Side by side they visit God's church and partake of God's Banquet; side by side they face difficulties and persecution, and share their consolation. They have no secrets from one another; they never shun each other's company; they never bring sorrow to each other's hearts."[46]

Biblical Application and Practical Study

1. Plan a surprise date night for your spouse (search the Internet for helpful tips on creative date nights).

2. Do this communication exercise: Write down 3-5 topics for discussion (serious or fun) and put

in a bowl/hat in the middle of the table. Sit at opposite ends of the table so you can look directly at one another. Take turns pulling a paper from the bowl. After reading the topic, the person that pulls the paper gets to start the conversation. Do not interrupt! Then give your spouse a chance to respond with no interruptions. Once the topic is "dead" pick a new piece of paper.

3. Study James 5:15-16, Proverbs 28:13, and Matthew 18:15. Journal about what you learn. Write personally about these thoughts:
    - Realize that conflicts are inevitable; therefore expect them.
    - Realize that conflicts are sinful; therefore resolve them.
    - Realize that conflicts are opportunities; therefore use them.[47]

4. Study and memorize Matthew 7:3-5. What are you focusing on in your spouse and neglecting to see in your own life?

5. Read Matthew 18:15 and 5:23-26. According to the Bible, whose responsibility is it to seek reconciliation?

Section Three: Addictions

Chapter Six

Addiction's Downward Spiral

But each person is tempted when he is lured and enticed by his own desire. Then desire when it has conceived gives birth to sin, and sin when it is fully grown brings forth death. Do not be deceived, my beloved brothers.
James 1:14-16

"Try Harder!" Often when it comes to addiction, we may not voice it, but those words pop into our heads. Or you may be familiar with the *Saturday Night Live* skit with Bob Newhart and Mo Collin, "Stop It!"

If only it were that easy.

Scripture sheds light on the truth of addiction, "Don't you know that when you offer yourselves to someone [or something] to obey him as slaves, you are slaves to the one whom you obey" (Romans 6: 16). Licensed psychologist and the Director of Counseling at the Christian Counseling and Education Foundation, Dr. Edward Welch, echoes Scripture explaining that addiction feels like something—a virus—has taken over and you are no longer in control. To just say "no" may seem effective to the person who has never been captured by addictions, but it is a joke to those who have fallen victim to it.[48]

No person chooses to become an addict, but as sin never satisfies and always requires "more"—a person becomes an addict after being captivated by sin over and over again.

To give a more formal definition, addiction is "bondage to the rule of a substance, activity, or state of mind, which then becomes the center of life, defending itself from the truth so that even bad consequences don't bring repentance, and leading further estrangement from God."[49]

Many people focus on the aspect of disease when speaking of addiction, perhaps because it makes the problem more palatable. In this model, the addict—who is responsible for his hurtful actions toward others—has inherited a disease that stimulates the addiction. Therefore, in a way, addicts are released from the accountability for their own sinful choices that *conceived* the addiction. In this model, the addict is never healed, always an addict. If we accept the disease model, then there is no true freedom! Christ can free any addict from the emotional *and* physiological problems surrounding addiction.

Thankfully, Scripture is clear. In Christ, true healing and eternal change are possible! Though we are warned: A deadly disease is ravishing body and soul: sin. All of us have the potential to become addicts. As we become slaves to the things we worship, those things rule over us. There is a greater problem with addiction then a chemical imbalance or a hereditary gene.

Biochemistry can definitely play a role in addiction, yet it is not the most destructive factor.

The Sin Problem

The predominant problem humanity wrestles with on earth is sin. All problems stem from this one issue of sin. Sin indwells in our nature, and sin multiplies through a fallen creation. Sin is missing the mark, the twisted betrayal of evil desires or deeds toward the Creator God. At its basis, the essence of sin is idolatry. Therefore, every sin committed constitutes a desire to worship someone or something in the place of God.

Sin began with Satan's defiance toward God, and continues through Satan as the ruler of the world and humanity's sinful nature or fleshly desires. Humans are evil sinners. We are all totally depraved. Even our righteous acts are like filthy rags before God. This might sound terribly bleak, but shows us our desperate need for a glorious Savior! Sin's attractiveness is that it delivers self-gratification every time. But sin is also ruthlessly deceptive. It promises pleasure but never—not ever—fully satisfies (2 Corinthians 11:14-15).

Sinful Heart and Thoughts Cause Pain

Problems start in the heart. These heart problems lead to unbiblical deeds, which are normally accompanied with bad feelings. So what is the heart?

According to Scripture, the heart is equated with the location of belief and faith.[50]

Only God can accurately judge the spiritual condition of the heart, but feelings often indicate whom we desire to worship, God or self. If sinful thoughts are left to fester, they often become sinful actions. Psalm 32:3-4 explains this concept: "When I kept silent, my bones wasted away through my groaning all day long. For day and night your hand was heavy on me; my strength was sapped as in the heat of summer." Even for the believer, emotions that emerge through unbiblical thoughts bring up pain. By dwelling on these thoughts, we forget that we have been forgiven in Christ. Forgetfulness of God's grace, mercy, and blessing is one of the gravest consequences of addiction.

The View of Self through the Lens of Sin

The ubiquitous nature of Facebook is mind-boggling. Millions of people spend hours posting and reading posts daily. I admit…I have a Facebook account. There is one thing I hate about Facebook, besides the amount of wasted hours God is going to hold us accountable for one day. I hate the perfectly depicted lives of every person listed (I'm no exception). Beautiful pictures, laughter, happy children, parties—no one posts *real* life! Ever. No one has a bad hair day, and no one posts snapshots of yelling matches between spouses or kids. I think Facebook is an international scam. Onlookers can become jealous, receiving a falsified report of our lives. However, it gives us a great picture of how we view ourselves when blinded by sin.

Through the lens of sin, our bad choices become acceptable with little or no consequence. Sin blinds us from real life, a living God, and the reality of painful consequences, so much in fact, that we begin seeing our world as a fantasy. It is picture perfect, just the way we want it to look. We are in control (and can stop anytime), everything is fine, and nothing we are doing is hurting others or ourselves. Every day is a good hair day!

The truth is simple. Sin blinds us from seeing its devastating effects. The way we feel and how we view ourselves, relationships, and circumstances are often indications of whether we are living to please God or ourselves. John Owens laments, "Every unmortified sin will certainly do two things; first, it will weaken the soul, and deprive it of its vigour; secondly, it will darken the soul, and deprive it of its comfort and peace."[51] A consistent blinding by sin and a world of constant fantasy—it's a breeding ground for addiction. And the consequences are ruthless.

The Failure of Behavior Modification

In the world of addictions, behavior modification is one of the most practiced counseling methods in residential and outpatient treatment centers, whether secular or religious. Most of these models are rooted in Western individualistic culture, claiming when needs are not met, problems ensue.

According to these models, the addict fills his or her void with an unacceptable behavior according to societal norms (i.e. sex, drugs, alcohol). This addict needs a new set of behaviors that are more acceptable and helpful. Behavior modification is the process by which the addict shifts unacceptable behaviors to more acceptable behaviors because the positive benefits of the new behaviors outweigh the negative effects of the old behaviors. Once the addict learns to pursue these new behaviors, he or she will change.

The problem is that behavior modification often does not work as well as most would like. The success rate hovers around 20 percent for addicts in rehab programs. Therefore, changing behaviors and (willing it to stick) is not working for many people. In the 1960s, biblical counseling rose in prominence. Practitioners encouraged the local church once again to be the beacon of hope, lifting high the Word of God as the authority.

Biblical counseling is founded on the perspective that a person's worldview forms the course of his or her thoughts, speech, and behavior. That is why Scripture is so robust, teaching Christians to train their thoughts and hearts to be gospel-centered and eternally-focused. The goal of counseling must not simply be behavioral change, but rather life-change, down to the very root of the heart.

Motivation for Change

Only through Christ's grace becoming real in your life will you be motivated for practical change. Only the gospel can help you to face the pressures and responsibilities of life, to learn to love others, and to give God glory in everything you do. By living in the power of the Spirit, only then can you put to death all idols and worship God with a pure heart.

Behavior modification *cannot* transform you because it is based on self-will. That same self-will says, "I want to stop, but I can't!" Behavior modification offers no true heart change. Only the gospel of Jesus Christ can free you from the enslavement of addiction.

The Gospel's Power in Transformation

Repentance is more than feeling sorry for sin or asking forgiveness. It is not just mental. It is behavioral. It is turning from sin. This behavior must be rooted in true heart change. Biblical change begins with your spiritual birth and continues throughout your life.

The purpose for living changes from a focus of living for self to one of dying to self, learning to love God and love others in a biblical manner.[52] New thoughts and behavior will only lead to change if empowered by the Holy Spirit living in you. Christianity is not based on works, and behaviors must not be the focus of change. A plea of "just help me stop feeling like this" may or may not be a true desire for change. Check your motivations. Do you desire to change because of your realization of something greater than self-worship, or are you simply tired of feeling bad?

A Call to Obey

To have faith in Christ means you don't shrink from his commands. Missionary George Peters said, "Whatever else cross-bearing may mean, it certainly implies such voluntary identification with the Lord that he absorbs our love, devotion, time, talent and strength to such a degree that nothing and no one else matters in our life except the Lord."[53] Is that your cry now? Living God's way means putting away our self-centeredness and committing ourselves to follow God's Word *in the power of the Spirit*, in spite of any feelings to the contrary. It is a choice, an action.

First John 15:10-11 explains, "If you keep my commands, you will remain in my love, just as I have kept my Father's commands and remain in his love. I have told you this so that my joy may be in you and that your joy may be complete." The Word of God is crucial for lasting true change. And a life covenanted to Christ is crucial for a joyous fulfilled life!

Right Living Empowered by the Spirit

Apart from the basic tenants of the Christian faith, there is no guideline for right living. The Holy Spirit empowers change in leading us to salvation and working in our sanctification. The evidence of the Spirit's fullness in our lives is clearly presented in Scripture (Ephesians 5:18-21). All Christians are commanded to be full of the Spirit. According to Scripture, the Holy Spirit is seen in a true Christian's fruit, namely self-control. Those filled with the Spirit must use their mind, and act in an intelligent, controlled, healthy relationship with God.

The Spirit's fullness involves not a private, mystical experience but rather a moral relationship with God and others. The Holy Spirit manifests in the Christian's life through proper Christ-directed worship and submissive fellowship with God and the church body. John MacArthur aptly explains, "As a divinely indwelling teacher, the Spirit of Truth fills a function that no human counselor or mental health professional can even approach. He is constantly there, pointing the way to truth, applying the truth directly to our hearts, prompting us to conform to the truth—in short, sanctifying us in the truth."[54]

Scripture reveals, "No temptation has overtaken you except what is common to mankind. And God is faithful; he will not let you be tempted beyond what you can bear. But when you are tempted, he will also provide a way out so that you can endure it" (1 Corinthians 10:13; Titus 2:11-14, 3:4). Once you have the power of the Spirit guiding you—though temptations still attack—you can say "NO!" Do we believe this?

A New Model for Addiction, Rooted in Truth

Our worldview will be the catalyst that drives the course of our lives. If our identity and purpose changes, then our thoughts, speech, and behavior will also change. If we only teach the addict a new set of socially acceptable behaviors to avoid legal or relational problems, he or she will preserve the original desire to serve and worship self for pleasure and fulfillment. And the root problem remains unchanged.

A person who claims to believe and follow Jesus Christ will have evidence of this new life transformation. He or she will have resources to fight! From Scripture we know that "no higher knowledge, no hidden truth, nothing besides the all-sufficient resources that we find in Christ exist that can change the human heart."[55]

This new life will be full of the Spirit. This new life sheds fleshly pursuits. This new life includes reliance on the Word of God, humble prayer, the pursuit of fellowship with other believers, and a bold gospel witness. How we purify our hearts according to Scripture is not by condemning ourselves or resolving to mend our ways by doing penance or behaving a certain way, but by asking for help from an outside rescue. We escape to the love of Jesus Christ through the powerful work of the Holy Spirit.

Lasting transformation comes from the work of Jesus Christ, not from humanity's philosophies and methods. As the gospel changes men and women who have been addicted to a life-dominating sin, the culture of mental health will be introduced to and changed by the true Professional.

Isaiah writes, "Forget about what's happened; don't keep going over old history. Be alert, be present. I'm about to do something brand-new" (Isaiah 43:18).

Friend if you are addicted . . . today is the day of freedom! Turn to Christ, be filled with the Spirit, and ask the church to help carry your burdens. The fight will be hard, at times the losses may seem great, but victory will be yours!

Biblical Application and Practical Study

1. What are you currently enslaved to? Write out your own definition of addiction and addict. Include your personal sin strongholds.

2. Study and memorize Titus 2:11-14, 3:4-7 and 1 Corinthians 10:12-13. What does these verses mean? How should you respond to your personal strongholds?

3. Read Proverbs 1-9 (look closely at what Folly leads to and what Wisdom leads to). Read Colossians 2-3 and James 1:14-15, 4:1-10.

4. Read *Appendix C: A Study Psalm 63:1-8 and Titus 2-3:8*.

CHAPTER SEVEN

REBELLING MY WAY

So I find it to be a law that when I want to do right, evil lies close at hand. For I delight in the law of God, in my inner being, but I see in my members another law waging war against the law of my mind and making me captive to the law of sin that dwells in my members. Wretched man that I am! Who will deliver me from this body of death? Thanks be to God through Jesus Christ our Lord!
Romans 7:21-25

Biblical change begins with spiritual rebirth and continues as a process of sanctification throughout your life. Every person in the world encounters various trials throughout life. You are not alone.

Addiction not only targets unbelievers. As crises arise and strips Christians of their joy, spiritual amnesia of the resources to overcome temptations and trials often occurs. The truth is many Christians who claim Jesus as Lord fall to sin's enslavement.

Life is a battle!

Our enemy seeks to defeat us by tempting us to trust in our own wisdom, to live according to our self-centered feelings, and to gratify the desires of our flesh.

In contrast, God's will is for us to be victorious in all of these tests for his honor and glory.[56] God's tests strengthen his children's commitment to him. In that regard, tests are for our good (Romans 15:4). However, Satan uses temptations for evil, to "seduce each child away from his devotion to Jesus Christ" (2 Corinthians 11:3). Let's look at a case study about a Christian man who was enticed, seduced, and enslaved by the enemy.

Eric: A Case Study

Married for nine years, Eric and Amanda have a relationship that seems to glorify God. From the time they began dating they worked hard to establish a godly relationship, focusing on Christ's guidance for all of their decisions and dreams. They even waited to kiss until their wedding day.

Members of a strong, Bible-believing church, participants in a weekly Bible study, and serving in multiple church ministries, Eric and Amanda thought they were working hard to build an impenetrable marriage.

Both Eric and Amanda spent time in the Word every morning, studying, praying, and seeking godly lives. They would even admit to having great communication and a very fulfilling sex life. To their friends and family, they were carefree and had the kind of romance everyone hopes for.

The Confession

About a year-and-a-half into their marriage, Eric confessed to Amanda that he was looking at pornography. It began when he was introduced to porn as an adolescent. He allowed it to continue into their marriage. She knew that he had struggled with pornography before they were married, but he promised that he would not dishonor her with it again. He was ashamed and thought he could confess it to God, be forgiven, and move on without telling her. Being tortured with guilt by his lack of confession, statements of faithfulness, and continual struggle, Eric realized withholding this information was lying to Amanda. After a godly mentor instructed him to confess this sin to his wife, Eric heeded the advice. For Amanda, it was not only the unfaithfulness of pornography that hurt, it was also the betrayal of being lied to for so long. She was devastated.

After receiving counsel from an older couple, Amanda forgave Eric—pleading with him to communicate with her even about things most vulnerable. Slowly they grew in their relationship and Amanda reestablished her trust in Eric. Four years went by with great excitement: growth in the Lord, a stronger marriage, a baby, a new location, and graduate school. Safety measures were enforced to protect their marriage from the temptation and destruction of pornography. They installed computer software, found another great church in their new location, got involved in a Bible study, and met with other men and women weekly for accountability. Their marriage seemed to be stronger than ever and they were asked to be leaders in their church.

One afternoon while Eric was away at work, Amanda reviewed the computer software report. To her disbelief, she saw pornographic sites listed among others banned from the computer. Since they had been out of town the weekend before, she thought the friend who was watching their house was the offender. Frantic for Eric to help his friend, Amanda called her husband during his lunch break and asked him to confront his friend. He assured her he would. After Eric came home from work that evening, he told Amanda the truth.

It was not his friend who was looking up these websites, it was him. Eric admitted to embracing the temptation and succumbed to dishonor God and her. Eric could not explain why he did it; he just did. He wanted to rebel.

His Bible study was suffering. He didn't feel close to God, and he was having a difficult time in grad school—so he welcomed this temptation as an escape from his current anxieties. Not only was Amanda more hurt, confused, and betrayed than before, Eric was broken. How could he stop this sin-cycle? He was already a Christian who desired to honor the Lord and be faithful to his wife and family. He knew this sin could destroy his marriage and his current ministry. He knew after all the attempts to squash this sin. He never truly gave it over to the Lord. It was time to die to self and live for Christ.

From Faithful to Failure: Embracing Temptation

Eric is a man who truly loves the Lord and desires to glorify him. So how did he go from faithfulness to failing in his sinful thoughts and actions? "Satan uses three attractions of the world—the lust of flesh (gratification of desires), the lust of the eyes (coveting), and the boastful pride of life (self-centered living)—as an enticement for people to do evil. His diabolic efforts are designed to seduce believers away from their devotion to Jesus Christ so they will gratify their lusts and selfish desires (2 Corinthians 11:3; James 1:13-15)."[57] However, Scripture says Satan is a liar, and the way of the world only leads to destruction.

Eric admitted to his accountability partner and his wife that the reasons behind his rebellious sin was his lack of intimate time spent with God, his lackadaisical attitude towards school work and Bible study, and feeling like the world's way was easier and more desirable at the moment, but mainly, his wrong understanding of the fear of God.

Embracing Versus Resisting

Temptation involves both doing and feeling, which are heart issues. Falling to temptation causes serious consequences to a believer's relationship with

God. Eric realized this when he felt like he needed to gratify the flesh. Failure at the doing level was evidenced when Eric listened to Satan instead of God, causing him to hide in his sin. Eric decided, as he did the first time he looked at pornography at the beginning of his marriage, that confessing his sin to God was "good enough" since he did not want to tell anyone else, especially Amanda. This decision only led to a broken relationship with God and his wife.

Failure at the feeling level and doing level reveal the failure at the heart level, which is directed at pleasing self instead of pleasing God. Instead of believing the lies, as a believer Eric should have relied on Jesus' example to combat temptation. However, he was not in close relationship with God and allowed Satan a foothold. Jesus' resistance to temptation and his defeat of Satan gives all believers hope. Remember, Jesus "has been tempted in every way, just as we are—yet was without sin. [Therefore we can] approach the throne of grace with confidence, so that we may receive mercy and find grace to help us in our time of need" (Hebrews 4:15-16).

Temptations Leading to Sin

Temptations are a type of trial, but different from the emotional or physical pain we cannot prevent. From James we get a definition of both trials and temptations: "Blessed is the man who perseveres under trial, because when he has stood the test, he will receive the crown of life that God has promised to those who love him. When tempted, no one should say, 'God is tempting me.' For God cannot be tempted by evil, nor does he tempt anyone; but each one is tempted when, by his own evil desire, he is dragged away and enticed."[58] A conquered trial leads to blessing. A coveted temptation leads to evil. God is the initiator of trials to build our faith. Satan is the initiator of temptations to destroy our faith.

Why is Sin So Alluring?

Satan masks himself and his work as good. Not often do we engage in sin that we believe will end in death (whether spiritually or physically). We don't think, "If I smoke crack I will get addicted, ruin my life, and die early from overdose." Or "I will engage in an extramarital affair, destroy my family, and ruin my life in the process." But Satan, watching and learning our weaknesses, lures us in by his façade of sin and our fleshly desires to embrace it.

Here is how sin works. We see with our eyes that it looks good and pleasing, then we reach out and taste just a little, soon it becomes our desire of choice until we feast upon it. We can't get enough, and slowly it dulls our senses. We need more of it...more or maybe something even better, different this time. Nothing seems to quench the desires that rattle our body—we are consumed. We start to ask ridiculous questions. Can this really be sin if I desire it so much? Doesn't God want me to be happy? Can God really fulfill my desires?

Satan is the Deceiver

From the very beginning, we see the story unfold: creation, Adam and Eve, and the fall of humanity through sin. In the beginning God designed all of creation for one purpose. He created the heavens and the earth, animals, and humans to bring him glory! He also promised to bless Adam and Eve as they ruled and subdued the earth together, ultimately to give God all glory. However, they choose to doubt God and believe the serpent. They thought God might be holding something back, something greater.

They believed that God did not love them enough to fulfill all their desires and needs. So, even though they had union with God and a blessing from God, they thought something other than God could give them more. When they embraced that something, it destroyed them. This same sin exists today, and it continues to destroy people.

When we embrace sin, we believe sin is true fulfillment. When in actuality only following God brings true fulfillment. Sin is a smoke screen. It imitates something good, perverts it. Once you break through this façade, you see it for what it really is: a lie. God is Creator of all. He knows what we truly need.

When Satan deceives us, we have the choice to embrace or flee sin. Do you believe God is who he claims? Do you believe the Bible is the very words of God? Do you really believe God knows what's best for you—his beloved?

The Heart: The Root of Sin

In the last chapter we learned that problems begin in the heart and lead to unbiblical deeds, such as a temptation to follow fleshly desires instead of a commitment to God. This wrong path may result in bad feelings—depression, despair, or guilt. Let's look back at our case study. Eric's sin did not begin when he turned on the computer. It began with his lustful heart that did not believe that God is who He claims to be, to be feared above all else, or that He knew what was most fulfilling for Eric. We can echo the Psalmist who praised God: "You make known to me the path of life; in your presence there is fullness of joy; at your right hand are pleasures forevermore!" (Psalm 16:11). Choosing God's way is not settling for something lesser! It is fully experiencing—body and soul—perfect pleasures, unhindered by guilt, shame, consequences.

Eric realized he lived a self-centered life, pleasing his own fleshly desires instead of living a life of God-centeredness. He realized his "trigger" to this sin was his wrong understanding of the fear of God. Eric knew he needed to direct his thoughts away from self and toward pleasing God—because God is worthy of praise. Until Eric personally felt the disgust of this sin, it would still have an appeal. Slowly, he began a life process of biblical change.

Freedom in Christ from Sin's Power

In Christ we are freed from the power and penalty of sin. The feeling of being controlled by sin will come with temptation, but the truth is there is nothing that can separate us from the love of God. The Apostle Paul said in Romans 7, "I know that nothing good lives in me, that is, in my sinful nature." He calls himself a "wretched man" and asks, "Who will rescue me from this body of death?" His answer: "Thanks be to God—through Jesus Christ our Lord." Remember Peter? He cursed Jesus, God the Son, directly to his face. Can there be a greater sin? Could you image the guilt and shame? After that hateful betrayal of Peter, Jesus marched to Calvary, became shame and took guilt to its death! The cross of Jesus is available for all to embrace perfect forgiveness—no shame, no guilt. No sin is too great.

The Bible says, because of our relationship with Jesus, our "old self has been crucified with him, so that the body of sin (our sinful nature) might be done away with, that we should no longer be slaves to sin—because anyone who has died has been freed from sin."[59] That doesn't mean temptations cease to come or we are no longer sinful—not until we enter heaven. But it does mean that "when you are tempted to sin, God will provide a way out so you can stand up under it" (1 Corinthians 10:13). God gives believers his grace and strength to endure every test and resist every temptation so that you never have to sin.[60] We have the power!

Finally, do not lose sight. When you confess your sins, God forgives and cleanses you. When you confess your sins to God and develop a pattern of recognizing sin and dealing with it God's way, you acknowledge his Lordship. This enables you to have unhindered communication with the heavenly Father, a fruitful prayer life. And when you consistently confess your sins to others, you encourage harmonious relationships. Demonstrate the difference that Jesus makes in your life.

Biblical Application and Practical Study

1. Read Romans 5-8. Focus on Romans 7:21-25. Paul explains the battle between our sin nature and the Spirit living within us. Where is our hope for victory found?

2. Write yourself a letter expressing the truth found in Romans 5-8. Explain in detail who you were before Christ changed you, what happened when you gave your life to Christ, how you are to live in freedom as a Christian, what 'Christ as Lord' means, and the power you have to conquer sin. Encourage yourself that in Christ, "we are more than conquerors!"

3. Memorize Romans 8:37.

4. Write yourself notes of biblical truth and scripture verses that you post throughout the day to help you fight your sin stronghold. Some examples for posts could be: mirrors, car dashboards, computer keys, phone, desk at work, rooms in house, and refrigerator.

5. See *Appendix C: A Study on Ephesians 1*

Chapter Eight

Fulfilled God's Way

Let not sin therefore reign in your mortal body, to make you obey its passions. Do not present your members to sin as instruments for unrighteousness, but present yourselves to God as those who have been brought from death to life, and your members to God as instruments for righteousness. For sin will have no dominion over you, since you are not under law but under grace.
Romans 6:12-14

Eric was fearful that his self-centered actions may cost his marriage. He also feared his leadership at church could be suspended or ended. Though in God's overflowing mercy, He did not allow severe consequences to hinder Eric, but disciplined him through tough accountability time, his own Bible study, and the Christ-like forgiveness from his wife, all of which humbled and taught Eric to properly love and fear God.

In great wisdom from Eric's church leadership, he learned "in order to put off the old sinful habits, you must first identify them by examining (judging) your life in light of God's Word, confess them, and immediately put them aside."[61]

Eric began judging his life in view of God's standard, not his own. He realized he was not living according to Philippians 4:8, which says, "whatever is true, whatever is noble, whatever is right, whatever is pure, whatever is lovely, whatever is admirable—if anything is excellent or praiseworthy—think about such things." Eric determined to practice that verse. He put on righteous deeds in the power of the Holy Spirit[62] and he glorified God by demonstrating his love for him. Eric learned true repentance.

Lasting and Effective Biblical Change

We must realize effective and lasting biblical change is an ongoing process. We are to obey the commands and guidelines in God's Word for every area of your life (thoughts, words, and actions).[63] Eric's sin not only hurt his witness as a Christian, but also led his wife into an active battle with her sin of self-righteousness. Amanda even doubted Eric's salvation, not understanding how a man who loved the Lord as he said he did could *seek out* sin. Eric knew he needed to take steps toward biblical change so he could restore his relationship with his wife, but most importantly, to learn how to truly glorify his God.

Steps of Change

First, Eric committed himself to God's sovereignty and rule in his life. He trusted in Jesus as his

Lord and Savior when he was young, but he needed to determine to live each day in a posture that pleased God.[64]

Second, Eric "determined specific ways he sinned against God and confessed these sins to him." God's Word explains that "he who conceals his sins does not prosper, but whoever confesses and renounces them finds mercy" (Proverbs 28:13).

Third, Eric asked God for wisdom to know what changes to make and how to make them, asking with faith that He would answer. Then he confessed his specific sins to those he sinned against, mainly his wife, by his words and actions. Eric decided to study God's Word on a regular basis and memorize Scripture to store God's truth in his heart. He was determined to pray unceasingly. And he would *do* what God says in his Word regardless of his feelings in order to glorify God. All this was possible guided by the Holy Spirit.

Renewing Your Mind

Eric knew from Scripture that he needed to renew his mind. Paul admonishes in Romans, "do not conform any longer to the pattern of this world, but be transformed by the renewing of your mind. Then you will be able to test and approve what God's will is—his good, pleasing and perfect will." [65] As you put off the old continuing pattern of sin and put on the new practice of righteousness and holiness, you are renewed in the spirit of your mind.[66] Hearing the Word through the life of the church, reading the Word, studying the Word, memorizing the Word, and mediating on the Word, was quickly put into practice. Eric then had opportunities for the Word of Christ to dwell richly within him.

Satan tempts repeatedly and continually, which Eric learned even after making these changes. He needed to be on guard! Eric learned he could resist Satan's onslaughts by cooperating with God's plan to renew his mind. Salvation is the first step to this process, which Eric already had. Secondly, he would be obedient to God's Word, insuring his mind to continue increasing in Christlikeness.

As a result of renewing his mind, soon Eric learned that continual obedience to the Word of God protects you from delusion and increases your spiritual discernment and sensitivity to sin.

Plan of Action against Temptation

Making biblical changes in your life requires prayerful and purposeful action. To respond immediately to his need for biblical change, Eric developed a basic plan for living a changed life on a daily basis. He keeps the computer locked at all times, only using the computer when Amanda is home. He developed a contingency plan to deal immediately with temptation when it occurs (1 Peter 5:8-9). When struggling with lust: (1) Contact Amanda first; (2) Call either of his accountability partners; (3) Pray for his wife, pray for his children never to be mistreated by a man, and pray for the women on pornography sites to know Christ; (4) Review scripture memory verses to focus on God's truth of conquering sin; and (5) pray to God for sin to be conquered.

Eric would also establish open communication with Amanda, being vulnerable about his sin, not just lust, but also any time a struggle or temptation presented itself. Besides times of solitude with the Lord daily, Eric sought opportunities to serve within the church and beyond, and work to evangelize the lost—focusing on others instead of himself.

Hope in the Midst of Trials

Eric found hope in the midst of crisis because he learned that those in Christ are freed from the *power* and penalty of sin. Pornography is a sin that is accompanied by a *feeling* of full-body possession. Eric learned that though the *feeling* of being controlled by it may still come with the temptation, the *truth* is that nothing can separate him from the love of God. Temptations have no power over him. God gives believers his grace and strength to endure every test and resist every temptation.[67]

Another encouraging hope Eric clings to is the truth that when you confess your sins, God forgives and cleanses you. Eric received God's peace when he confessed his sin and put on righteousness. Finally, Eric was not only given God's hope and peace, he was also given a restored relationship with God and his wife.

I can happily report that Eric continues to practice the biblical steps to change, realizing that change is a life process of obedient living. He is careful not to think he is standing firm against lust because God's Word is clear that in those prideful moments it is easiest to fall (1 Corinthians 10:12). However, he praises the Lord for a deeper, more intimate relationship with Him and also his wife, who forgave him and loves him more every day. God in his awesome work used this temptation to discipline his son and bring him back into a restored relationship with him. What a mighty God who conquers temptation and sin!

Biblical Application and Practical Study

1. Write your story. Begin with how you grew up, when you came to know Jesus as Savior and Lord, how you failed and grew, what major lessons you have learned, the milestones of your life, where you are currently in life and with the Lord, and explain your future desires and dreams.

2. Read Psalm 51. Write your own lament for sin, pleading with God to cleanse your heart. After, read Psalm 103 and have a time of worship (writing, singing, praying, etc.) expressing to God thanksgiving for His promise to cleanse

your heart and forgive all sin in Christ! (This is a great activity to do when serious about fighting your sin stronghold. Have a counselor or accountability partner aware of the completion of this assignment.)

3. See *Appendix C: A Study on 2 Peter 2:2-11*

4. Make an action plan to battle sin. See *Appendix D* for examples. (This includes finding mature accountability partners).

Section Four: Restoration

CHAPTER NINE

THE POWER OF TRANSFORMATION

Do not be conformed to this world, but be transformed by the renewal of your mind, that by testing you may discern what is the will of God, what is good and acceptable and perfect.
Romans 12:2

Jesus is our motivation to transform into someone glorious. God, through the Holy Spirit, often uses other believers, the Bible, prayer, and life experiences to mold us into his image. My hope is that you find other believers who will hold you accountable in the transformation changes God is asking you to make.

Transformation: The Local Church

As God ushered in the New Covenant under the reign of Christ, he commissioned the local church to be the refuge for believers—encouraging one another with the Word of God so that no one would be hardened by sin's deceitfulness. The local church became the God-ordained assembly, those called the family of God, to provide material provisions and spiritual encouragement for every believer. The best way for the Christian to avoid failure and carry burdens is in the fulfillment of the two great commandments to love God and neighbor.

In recent years, there has been a movement that gathering as the church is not necessary for a believer. This so-called movement is not biblical. Christ has commanded his followers to love his bride and continue meeting together for encouragement and protection. A great gauge on whether we love Christ at all is whether we love his people in the church.

Transformation: The Authority of the Word

God speaks to us through the reading and preaching of his Word. Worshipers must read it, hear it, meditate on it, and obey it. Theologian John Frame insisted in our worship, "to recognize that when we hear or read the Word of God, we are encountering God Himself."[68]

All information and knowledge must be filtered through the lens of Scripture. Not only is Scripture useful for correction and training in righteousness, it is also active, penetrating the attitudes of our hearts—revealing our motivations and worship.[69] Relying on the power of God's inerrant Holy Word will assure biblical change in every area of life. The Bible is our ultimate authority of truth.

Spiritual Maturation Leads to Transformation

Humanity's "solutions" to our difficulties will ultimately fail because they do not deal with the source of our problems: our heart. God's solutions, as revealed in Scripture, go to the heart of the matter where permanent change is accomplished.[70]

Christian, we should be as *empty* vessels—cleansed of self and ready for an assignment. In comes God's flow of power and glory with the Word, the Spirit and prayer, and out flows our gracious spirits, loving and helping others while reflecting God's image. Faith is not only turning to Jesus, but also turning from sin. If we come to God claiming that we hate sin and desire to be rid of it through Jesus, then at the same time we must have the seriousness to forsake that sin. Otherwise, our confession is only words.[71]

Relationship with God

The most important life experience you have must be a relationship with God, through faith in the Savior and Lord Jesus Christ. Worshiping with your life in reverence and awe of God's great mercy and grace. Frame again asserts, "Faith is important to our entire relationship with God—and certainly to worship; genuine faith generates an emotion of expectancy in worship: we trust God to keep his promises, to meet with us, to bless us in accordance with the gospel, and to change our lives by the power of his Word."[72]

Loving Others in Christ

As you begin flourishing in Christ through godly repentance, faithful living, and joy in all circumstances, you can minister to others with the comfort you have been given by the Lord (2 Corinthians 1:3-4). No suffering is in vain; God will use it for his glory if we allow him to use us. Scripture tells us not to become weary in doing good, for at the proper time we will reap a harvest if we do not give up.

The point of the Great Commission is to make disciples who would surrender all for the Lord. We must remember that Jesus doesn't have two classes of disciple: those who abandon their lives to his service and those who don't. The call to discipleship is the same for all. The call to discipleship is a call to confess our allegiance to Jesus in the face of a hostile world—a broken world where suffering, in all different forms, targets all people. We are called to serve him and his mission, whatever the cost. To be a disciple is to be a disciple-maker.[73]

Hope that Fulfills

Without the gospel and without the process of sanctification, no one has hope for true change. John MacArthur outlines Scripture's view of hope explaining how hope produces joy that remains, even through the most difficult trials.

1. Hope produces perseverance (Romans 8:24-25).
2. Hope produces confidence (2 Corinthians 3:12; Philippians 1:20).
3. Hope produces effective ministry (2 Corinthians 4:8-18).
4. Hope produces greater faith and love (Colossians 1:4-5).
5. Hope produces consistency (1 Thessalonians 1:3).
6. Hope produces increased energy and enthusiasm (1 Timothy 4:10).
7. Hope produces stability (Hebrews 6:19).
8. Hope produces a more intimate relationship with God (Hebrews 7:19).
9. Hope produces personal purity (1 John 3:3).[74]

As you grow in your relationship with God, biblical hope is an application of your faith that supplies a confident expectation in God's fulfillment of his promises. Coupled with faith and love, hope is part of the abiding characteristics in a believer's life.[75]

Biblical hope means to remain steadfast while eagerly waiting on the Lord, even in adversity. Hope fuels longsuffering! And this hope is a gift of God's grace.

Peace That Surpasses Understanding

Peace is characteristic of the Kingdom of God and can be experienced—even in a crisis. This peace surpasses our comprehension. God's peace is the guardian of our hearts and minds. It is experienced through continual trust in him.

Joy That Lasts

Joy is similar. Lasting joy that comes from God must be rooted in God, his character, and his works. True joy is even experienced in midst of sorrows and distress.[76]

Pure Hearts for Eternal Purposes

Don't beat yourself up or resolve to mend your ways by doing penance or you will quickly find yourself back in the cycle of guilt and shame. Instead ask for help from an outside rescue. We escape to the love of Jesus Christ through the powerful presence of the Holy Spirit. Hymn writer, Katharina von Schlegel said, "Most of the noise in our souls is generated by our attempts to control the uncontrollable. We grasp after wind." Knowing that to be true of most humans, we must cling to truth that explains this momentary affliction is preparing us for an eternal weight of glory beyond all comparison, the hope of an eternity spent with Christ. Read Psalm 131; it overthrows the powers-that-be to establish the reign of him-who-is.[77]

Only through Christ's grace becoming real in our lives will we be motivated for practical change to face the pressures and responsibilities of life, to learn to love others, and to give God glory in everything we do. Through knowing God and living in the power of the Spirit, we can put to death all idols and worship God with a pure heart.

You Will be Transformed!

Believer, your hope is in the Lord! He causes all things in your life to work together for good as you continually respond in love, demonstrated as obedience, to him. Understanding and responding biblically to problems glorifies God while He further conforms you to the image of Jesus Christ.

"Life counts—all of it. Every moment is potentially an opportunity to be guided by God into his way of living. Every moment is a chance to learn from Jesus how to live in the kingdom of God."[78] Every moment is a decision to live a life that is joyously captivated by the God who wants you to flourish!

Biblical Application and Practical Study

1. Read John 17:17; Colossians 3:16; 1 Thessalonians 5:17; Psalm 27:17. How are we molded in God's image?

2. A great gauge on whether we love Christ is how we love the church. Read Acts 2; James 5:16; Romans 15:14; Hebrews 3:13. Do you think you love the church and make gathering with the

body a priority in your life? If not, what are some steps you can take to fulfill the commandment to love the church? If you do, how can you spur on friends and family members to join you at church?

3. As with anything we are passionate about, the more we know about it the easier to share with others our excitement. Do you spend time daily in the Word? Read Psalm 19, 2 Timothy 4:16-17, and Hebrews 4:12. The more time we spend getting to know our Savior God, the more we passionately want to share His Gospel with others. Make it a priority to know God and His Word. Schedule a daily, morning Bible Study (or whatever time works best for you).

4. Study Psalm 119 (you may want to use a commentary to assist you as you study)

5. Hope in testing matures believers into the image Christ. Read Romans 5:3-5; Romans 8:28-30; Deuteronomy 8:2, 5.

Chapter Ten

The Calmer of the Storm

Come to me, all you who are weary and burdened, and I will give you rest. Take my yoke upon you and learn from me, for I am gentle and humble in heart, and you will find rest for your souls. For my yoke is easy and my burden is light."
Matthew 11:28-30

Amazement. Fear. Confusion. When the crowds watched Jesus, they knew something was different about this man. He healed the blind, touched the leper, ate with prostitutes, quenched the thirsty, fed the hungry, and restored the hearts of the broken. Jesus Christ is no ordinary man. He is God.

J.I. Packer explains suffering this way: "The grace of God is love freely shown toward guilty sinners, contrary to their merit and indeed in defiance of their demerit. It is God showing goodness to persons who deserve only severity (God's wrath) and had no reason to expect anything but severity."[79] Think about the logic behind our suffering. Trial or temptation strikes causing pain. In God's perfect power and goodness He wants to use the pain for our good and his glory, because He created us and He knows what is best for us.

But we fight and we fight. *No, God, don't allow me to feel pain. Give me comfort, perfect peace. Don't use this for good because it's too bad. Don't teach me; free me. I deserve more!*

Again God reminds us, *in My perfect power and goodness, I sent you My only Son to carry the entire load of your sin and suffering to the cross.* His plan is not comfort in one circumstance, but to free us forever. Comfort for eternity! Jesus would put an end to pain and conquer the sting of death once and for all. Jesus would bring Perfect Peace.

Still, we fight and we fight. *No, God, that's not the way I want freed from suffering. I want relief this instant or I won't believe in you. Eternal life! Who cares about that now while I'm still alive? Give me comfort and rest, or I won't believe you are good or powerful.*

If we stop our fighting long enough to catch a glimpse at the infinite love of God, we will be amazed at a God who suffered to death so that we would never have to fear dying, teaches us to give over our burdens so that He can bear the pain for us, and heals our broken hearts even when confused and questioning him—God is always faithful. And from this faithful God, we learn about suffering.

Learn Suffering from Jesus Christ

Jesus lived a sinless life and died for our sins—our betrayal against God, our Father. Remember Romans 5:8, Jesus suffered and died for us while we were still sinners. Through Jesus' resurrection from death, He has not only conquered death and gave us a future hope, but He gives us the power to live this life to the glory of God (i.e. Resurrection power).

Jesus practiced the resources of the Spirit: He was obedient to God, He had constant communing with God through prayer, He meditated on Scripture, He even had a close group of God-fearing men to support him.

Likewise, we need to be emulating Jesus' life—being obedient to God, even when we want relief from our constant hurt. Listening to the Word of God instead of culture or what we think is biblical. We need to seek God's Word to find the answers, not fit God's word to give us the answers we want to hear. We need to meditate on Scripture. Memorize passages that will help you battle bitterness and anger, guilt and shame…passages about God's strength and power to get us through terrible storms. We need to cry out to God through constant prayer. And we need strong Christian brothers and sisters to encourage us and challenge us to live for the Lord within our local church.

Encouragement through His Example

The Son of God suffered in a way that honored God Almighty. In doing so, He led those enslaved to God's grace. How do we suffer as to honor God? Simply, the things we've already repeated over and over: Know the Word, cry out to God, be challenged by the Bible and do what it says, give God praise even in your pain, trust that He is in control, loves you, and knows what is best. Trials make our hearts vulnerable and moldable to listen to God. *When* we don't hear him—continue to seek him.

Then when people see us suffering like Christ, we explain that our happiness, contentment, or suffering isn't what life is all about. And in that moment, just as Jesus did—we lead those enslaved to God's grace.

Be Filled with Joy through His Victory

Our God is no failure! Jesus conquered death and is now with God Almighty! Though we face many trials, we can consider it pure joy, because we know that the testing of our faith develops perseverance. And perseverance must finish its work so that we may be mature and complete, not lacking anything. Remember, this earth is not our home. We are not mortal beings. Remember, we are all immortal beings on this earth facing an eternity.

Peter told us, "the God of all grace, who called you to his eternal glory in Christ, after you have suffered a little while, will himself restore you and make you strong, firm and steadfast."[80] We don't know what other suffering will come our way or if our present suffering will even end here on earth, but the joy of Jesus' victory is that one day when we are with him, it will end! Pray that through the power of the Spirit living in us, we will persevere until the end of our trial—however long that may be—and suffer for the glory of God.

A Personal Lesson

Preparing to speak at a women's event, the Lord led me to a previous journal entry I had written during a leadership retreat. As I turned to my journal, I read what I had written that Fall day: *Father, I feel like you have one major lesson for me that you have constantly been speaking to me through all my trials: Lose myself in You so that others can come to know you and gain eternal life! What if all my trials have been to teach me to trust you so that you can use me as a vessel to save the lost! You hear my prayers, my pleas, but in your silence you are training my heart to stop being inward focused on my pain, and to be others focused. You are teaching me to wait on you so I cling to you—desperate and dependent. The fears and brokenness I have are nothing compared to the losts' brokenness. They wait for someone to share truth, have their questions answered and empty hearts filled. Lord use me to be your vessel.*

Then I wrote down the major trials throughout my life to hear what God was saying:

1. *Death of a loved one:* Life is fleeting. We must know the Savior, Jesus Christ.

2. *Waiting for my husband* (my husband is my first boyfriend . . . we started dating when I was a sophomore in college): Trusting the Lord that He knows who is best for me to marry. One who will help me grow in the Lord and for me to be used to grow my future husband. *Dustin is immeasurably more than I could ever ask or imagine!*

3. *Sin struggles or being sinned against:* How jealous the Lord is for our complete love and devotion. How sin destroys vulnerability and communication with God and others.

4. *Financial strain:* The lost are spiritually bankrupt and can never make enough payments to earn their salvation. We are all dependent on the One who owns all things, including our lives.

5. *Miscarriage:* God created a perfect humanity. Sin corrupted it and caused death. Many have chosen not to know their source of life. They don't grow full term, and never know their Father. They are miscarried forever in eternity.

6. *Infertility:* Four years of being unable to have a healthy baby made me realize how our inward focus often causes infertile ministry, with no new births coming out of our relationships with lost people. In other words, we stop caring

about the lost enough to actually verbally share the truth of Jesus with them. There are very few relationships that are pregnant with the gospel.

7. *Health problems:* Physical pain or fears cause ultimate dependence on God. With restored health comes the energy and urgency to share Christ with others. The lost are dying every moment of every day. Each day they break down more physically and spiritually, not knowing the Great Physician. Even more so than our physical bodies, God desires to heal our spiritual bodies. God uses the medicine of the gospel to bring new life to dying bones!

The Storm is Calmed in Isaiah 43-46

God desires to calm all our storms. Thus says the L ORD, He who created you: *Fear not, for I have redeemed you; I have called you by name, you are mine. When you pass through the waters, I will be with you; and through the rivers, they shall not overwhelm you… For I am the L ORD your God, the Holy One of Israel, your Savior. "You are my witnesses," declares the L ORD, "and my servant whom I have chosen, that you may know and believe me and understand that I am he." Before me no god was formed, nor shall there be any after me. I, I am the L ORD, and besides me there is no savior. I, I am he who blots out your transgressions for my own sake, and I will not remember your sins. Remember this and stand firm, recall it to mind. I bring near my righteousness; it is not far off, and my salvation will not delay!*

Jesus and his Disciples from Mark 4:35-40

That day when evening came, he said to his disciples, "Let us go over to the other side." Leaving the crowd behind, they took him along, just as he was, in the boat. There were also other boats with him. A furious squall came up, and the waves broke over the boat, so that it was nearly swamped. Jesus was in the stern, sleeping on a cushion. The disciples woke him and said to him, "Teacher, don't you care if we drown?" He got up, rebuked the wind and said to the waves, "Quiet! Be still!" Then the wind died down and it was completely calm. He said to his disciples, "Why are you so afraid? Do you still have no faith?"

For the disciples, this was a life-threatening trial. The Sea of Galilee was 680 feet below sea level. Winds blowing across the land were intensified in the sea and often caused unexpected and violent storms. The disciples were being tossed places they didn't want to go and fearful they would drown in this crisis. But though all hope seemed lost, Jesus—our Creator God (Colossians 1)—in power spoke simple words to calm the storm.

"Quiet! Be still!" The disciples were saved.

Over 2000 years ago, a huge storm was raging against all humanity—we faced the greatest storm—the fury of God's wrath toward sinners. But, Jesus—Creator God—in power came to earth to stand in our place. He was physically beaten and hung on a cross as the sacrifice. He was fully drowned under the weight of God's wrath against sin.

And with the words, "It is finished," he calmed this great storm so that our hearts can forever, "Quiet! And Be Still."

Just as Christ said to the disciples in the fear of their storm, "Why are you afraid? Do you still have no faith?" He also asks us that same question.

He is our loving Father, the faithful Husband, the Suffering Servant that died for our betrayal. If we are his children, He has already calmed our greatest storm—never allowing us to drown in God's wrath. He promises also to be our strength and calm when we face unexpected and violent storms here on earth. He is still the one who says, "Why do you not have faith…trust me. Be Still. I am here."

Forever, Glory to God

Repeated as the theme of this book—*As you focus on the cross*, both the Suffering of Christ and the Power of his Spirit made alive in you, *you will be able to give God glory and praise through your suffering!*

We are promised that suffering will come and we know it is painful. Satisfaction will never be perfect here on earth—we await perfection in our True Home. But, in the arms of our beloved Father can we have contentment, joy, and hope. The promise is: He who began a good work in you will carry it on to completion until the day of Christ Jesus (Philippians 1:6). Never give up this fight—even in suffering—never. Dear friend, suffer well to the glory of God as you meditate on Christ's perfect and powerful work on the cross!

The seas have lifted up their pounding waves. Mightier than the thunder of the great waters, mightier than the breakers of the sea—the Lord on high is mighty (Psalm 93:3-4).

For God is sufficient in the *Storms of Life.*

Biblical Application and Practical Study

1. Write a poem or song expressing your gratitude and awe for God's mighty power in suffering.

2. How has God been sufficient in your storms of life? List your trials and how God used them for good or grew you through the process (even if you never understood why the trial needed to happen).

3. Reading through Jesus' life example of suffering well, what is the area you need to learn the most from Him: The Lesson from His Life, Encouragement through His Example, or to Be Filled with Joy Through his Victory?

4. Now finished with this book, what is the greatest truth you have learned? How will you begin practicing trusting God in the midst of emotional pain, broken marriages, and/or addiction?

APPENDIX A

Resources on the Theology of Suffering

A Theology of Suffering and Difficulty: Corporate and Personal Aspects by Michael E. Lewis

Conversation with Five Christian Thinkers by Molly Field James

How Long, Oh Lord?: Reflections of Suffering and Evil by D.A. Carson

In Earthen Vessels: A Biblical Theology of Suffering by Gerald Peterman and Andrew Schmutzer

John Piper Sermon Series on Suffering: http://www.desiringgod.org/sermons/by-series/job-five-sermons-on-suffering

Suffering and the Sovereignty of God by John Piper and Justin Taylor

The Roots of Sorrow: A Pastoral Theology of Suffering by Philippians C. Zylla

With Joyful Acceptance, Maybe: Developing a Contemporary Theology of Suffering in

Resources on Emotional Suffering

Besides Still Waters: Words of Comfort for the Soul y Charles H. Spurgeon and Roy H. Clarke

Be Still, My Soul by David Martyn Lloyd-Jones, D. A. Carson, J. I. Packer and Nancy Guthrie

CCEF Booklets: "Forgiving Others" by Timothy S. Lane and "Freedom from Resentment" by Robert D. Jones

Holding Onto Hope: A Pathway through Suffering to the Heart of God by Nancy Guthrie

On Death and Dying by Elisabeth Kubler-Ross

Putting Your Past in Its Place: Moving Forward in Forgiveness and Freedom by Stephen Viars

Running Scared: Fear Worry, and the God of Rest by Edward T. Welch

Night of Weeping: When God's Children Suffer by Horatius Bonar

Spiritual Depression by Martyn-Lloyd Jones

The Rare Jewel of Christian Contentment by Jeremiah Burroughs

Total Forgiveness by R. T. Kendall

Trusting God: Even When Life Hurts by Jerry Bridges

Unpacking Forgiveness: Biblical Answers for Complex Questions and Deep Wounds by Chris Brauns

Uprooting Anger: Biblical Help for a Common Problem by Robert D. Jones

When God Weeps: Why our Suffering Matters to the Almighty by Joni Eareckson Tada

Resources on Marriage

Peacemakers: A Biblical Guide to Resolving Personal Conflict by Ken Sande

Relationships: A Mess Worth Making by Timothy S. Lane and Paul David Tripp

Resolving Everyday Conflict by Ken Sande

Sacred Marriage by Gary Thomas

Shepherding a Child's Heart by Tedd Tripp

The Art of Marriage (video series) by Wayne Grudem

The Language of Love and Respect: Cracking the Communication Code with Your Mate by Dr. Emerson Eggrich

The Meaning of Marriage: Facing the Complexities of Commitment with the Wisdom of God by Timothy Keller

When Sinners Say I Do by Dave Harvey

Resources on Addiction

Addictions: A Banquet in the Grave by Edward T. Welch

Addiction: A Disorder of Choice by Gene M. Heyman

Blame it on the Brain? Distinguishing Chemical Imbalances, Brain Disorders, and Disobedience by Edward T. Welch

Instruments on the Redeemer's Hands: People in Need of Change Helping People in Need of Change by Paul David Tripp

The Addictive Personality: Understanding the Addictive Process and Compulsive Behavior by Craig Nakken

The Mortification of Sin by John Owen

You Can Change: God's Transforming Power for Our Sinful Behavior and Negative Emotions by Tim Chester

APPENDIX B

Using Scripture to Express Great Grief

Many counselees who are experiencing terrible suffering have a fear of trusting the Lord. They normally swing between two sides of expressing the emotions of suffering: (1) fear of expressing their emotions to God or (2) they angrily express all pain calling God's character into question. This scriptural exercise will help them express their emotions biblically. Laments help us to grieve and bring restoration as we rightly view God's attributes.

1. Choose a Psalm of Lament that explains how you are feeling. Some examples could be Psalm 3, 6, 13, 28, 42, 56, 73, 88* and 89* (*read these two Psalms together, because they most likely were written as a complete Psalm).

Psalm 42 (example)

My soul is downcast within me;
therefore I will remember you
from the land of the Jordan,
the heights of Hermon—from Mount Mizar.
⁷Deep calls to deep
in the roar of your waterfalls;

all your waves and breakers
have swept over me.

Why, my soul, are you downcast?
Why so disturbed within me?
Put your hope in God,
for I will yet praise him,
my Savior and my God.

2. After you find a lament that speaks to your suffering, answer the following questions:
    a. Why does this connect to me?
    b. What are the most helpful verses?
    c. What is the major struggle of the Psalmist at the beginning?
    d. What is the conclusion the Psalmist comes to at the end?
    e. What does this lament say about grief and God's character?

3. Write your own lament to express your grief.
    a. Include the introduction or cry to the Lord
    b. Express the problem (fears, frustration, burden, etc.)
    c. Finish with a claim of trust to the Lord

Spend time asking the Lord to help you trust him and thanking him for his loving and good character. (You may want to write out this prayer in a journal).

APPENDIX C

Identity Study: A Few Brief Questions to See Your Heart

1. What does your walk with the Great Sufferer, Jesus Christ, look like?
    a. If you don't have a strong relationship with God before a trial, don't expect your first impulse to be to go near to God.
    b. Are you putting God on trial because life is different than your expectations?

2. What do your relationships with others look like?
    a. Who are you pursuing most? The easy relationships or the hard ones?
    b. In those tough relationships, when we don't focus on the cross and suffer with Jesus, we miss God's grace to us and grow bitter (Hebrews 12:15).
    c. We need God's grace to suffer well. Some of you may need God's grace to actually forgive someone who has hurt you. Some of you may need God's grace to understand that you have been forgiven fully and forever by the blood Christ shed for you.

THE STORMS OF LIFE

- d. How is your relationship with your local church? How involved are you in small group of Sunday school class? God created the local church to be your daily support and encouragement.

3. How do you view yourself?
   a. In other words, where or in whom do you find your identity?
   b. Is it in the suffering? Do you see yourself as a victim? Has this pain become so familiar to you that you have defined everything you do through the hurt and pain?
   c. Do you see yourself freed by Christ and as Romans 8 says, "Co-heirs with Christ?" Suffering, but fulfilled in Christ.
   d. Are you identifying with his suffering so that you can honor God each day through your thoughts, words, and actions as the power of God lives through you?

4. Start today. Do you need to trust in the Only One who truly understands your suffering and can fill you with power to endure this trial? Or do you need to forgive someone? Or do you need to begin cultivating your relationship with the Lord

through Bible Study, prayer, and a local church body?

A Study on Psalm 63:1-8 and Titus 2-3:8

Journal anything that stands out to you and answer these three questions as you read:

Psalm 63
1. What does it mean to seek God earnestly?
2. How would it feel to thirst for God like you were in a desert?
3. What promise do you have when you cling to God?

Titus
1. What is the gospel message (v. 3:4-7)?
2. How does the gospel impact our life and those around us?

A Study on 2 Peter 1: 2-11

First: Answer these questions separately and then discuss together

1. Are you actively growing in the knowledge of who God is?
2. Do you live in peace because of your knowledge of God and his grace in your life?

3. Do you live in a way that prepares you for Christ's return or your entrance into the Kingdom?
4. Whose power must we have in order to fight the corruption in the world and in our hearts?
5. How do we understand grace and peace?
6. Practically, what might a greater understanding of grace and peace look like in our personal life and how we treat others?
7. What keeps us from being ineffective and unproductive in our walk with Christ?

Second: Complete a word study. How does Scripture define the following words in verses 5-7?

1. Give a biblical definition of faith, goodness, knowledge, self-control, perseverance, godliness, brotherly-kindness, and love.
2. When we don't have these qualities in our life, what happens besides being ineffective and unproductive in our walk with Christ? What happens to our understanding of grace?
3. When we do have these qualities, what are we like (also read James 1:22-25)?
4. Since eternity *with God* is our true home, what must be our focus while strangers on earth (read 1 Peter 2:10-12)?

A Study on Ephesians 1

Read and answer the following question.

1. What do verses 1-10 explain?
2. What does verses 11-14 mean about this seal guaranteeing our future with God?
3. How are we sealed and what does that accomplish in our future and earthly life (also read 2 Peter 1, 1 Corinthians 10:13).
4. What are we saying about Christ's rule if we think we cannot overcome a sin?
5. How must we test ourselves to know we are in the faith (read 2 Corinthians 13)?

Appendix D

Example Action Plan A: Thought Sin

1. Daily review the message of the cross to understand the gospel in my life so I offer grace and forgiveness to others.

2. Daily pursue to dispel the sin from my own life (the log) instead of focusing on other's sins (the speck). Never believe the lie that I am strong enough never to fall (1 Corinthians 10:12). Look for Satan's prowling (1 Peter 5:8)!

3. Daily get up at 6:00-6:30 to have a good (at least an hour) Bible study and prayer time.

4. Memorize one passage of Scripture each week. Recite on Sunday afternoons.

5. Study passages on trusting God (His character), pride, and self-righteousness.

6. Witness to someone each week: it may be evangelizing a co-worker or a stranger.

7. Be open and honest during your counseling sessions.

Example Action Plan B: Action Sin (i.e. Lust)

1. Do not turn on your computer when alone and use protective computer software.

2. When in the moment of struggle, call two accountability partners, review Scripture, and pray.

3. Be vulnerable and open with accountability partners and your spouse.

4. Seek out an older mentor within the church that can encourage a more mature and intimate relationship with God.

5. Have a devotional time every day.

6. Memorize Scripture each week (two small verses or a passage). Recite these verses every Sunday

7. Seek opportunities to serve within the church.

Sources

Introduction

[1] Romans 8:38-39, NIV

Chapter One

[2] Jerry Bridges. *Trusting God: Even When Life Hurts.* Colorado Springs: NavPress, 2008.
[3] 2 Corinthians 12:9-10, ESV
[4] Romans 8:18, 28-32, NIV
[5] Milton Vincent, The Gospel Primer: Learning to See the Glories of God's Love. (Bemidji: Focus Publishing, 2008), 31-32.
[6] Isaiah 26:3-4, NIV
[7] The Story: *The Story Workshop Edition*. Bloomington: Spread Truth Publishing, 2012.
[8] Tchividjian: Tullian Tchividjian, "'Scriptures Come to Life' during 20/20 Conference,"
http://wwwwbrnow.org/news/February-2012/%E2%80%98Scriptures-Com-to-Life%E2%80%99-during-20-20-conference.
[9] The Story: *The Story Workshop Edition*. Bloomington: Spread Truth Publishing, 2012.
[10] Romans 5:12, ESV
[11] Jeremiah 32:39-40, NIV
[12] 1 Peter 3:18, ESV
[13] The Story, 47.

Chapter Two

[14] 2 Peter 1:3, NIV
[15] Psalm 37:24, NIV
[16] Romans 10:9-10, ESV
[17] Jerry Bridges. *Trusting God: Even When Life Hurts.* (Colorado Springs: NavPress, 2008), back cover.
[18] Job 2:5, NIV
[19] John Wesley, *A Plain Account of Christian Perfection.* (New York: G. Lane and P.P. Sandford, 1844), 50.
[20] Jerry Bridges. *Trusting God: Even When Life Hurts.* (Colorado Springs: NavPress, 2008), 166-167.

Chapter Four

[21] J.C. Ryle, Do You Believe? A Question for 1861 (London: Wertheim, MacIntosh, & Hunt), 13.
[22] Psalm 37:7-10, NIV
[23] Romans 3:12-14, 23
[24] John 15:1-2, NIV
[25] Jay E. Adams, *Marriage, Divorce, and Remarriage in the Bible: A Fresh Look at What Scripture Teaches* (Grand Rapids: Zondervan, 1980), 23.
[26] Andreas J. Köstenberger, God, Marriage & Family: Rebuilding the Biblical Foundation (Yorba Linda, CA: Crossway Books, 2004), 45.
[27] See Matthew 28:18-20; 2 Corinthians 5:20; Ephesians 5
[28] http://www.adherents.com/largecom/baptist_divorce

.html

[29] Wayne Grudem. *Man as Male and Female in Systematic Theology* (England: Inter-Varsity Press, 1994), 455.

[30] Wendy Plump. *The New York Times*. "A Roomful or Yearning and Regret." Dec. 9, 2010.

[31] See Malachi 2:16; Mark 10:6-10; Luke 16:18; Ephesians 5:23-32; 1 Corinthians 7:11

[32] See Proverbs 2:16-17; Malachi 2:14

[33] Köstenberger, 86.

[34] Köstenberger, 86.

[35] Leviticus 26:15, 44, NIV

[36] Judges 2:1, NIV

[37] Daniel R. Heimbach, *Introduction to Christian Ethics: Lecture Note,* Southeastern Baptist Theological Seminary. 2009.

[38] Köstenberger, 229.

[39] See Matthew 5:32; Matthew 19:9; 1 Corinthians 7:15

[40] Samuele Bacchiocchi, *The Marriage Covenant: A Biblical Study on Marriage, Divorce, and Remarriage.* (Berrien Springs: Biblical Perspectives, 1992).

[41] Köstenberger, 257.

[42] John Murray, *Principles of Conduct: Aspects of Biblical Ethics* (Grand Rapids: William B. Eerdmans Publishing Company, 1957), 79.

Chapter Five

[42] Tertullian [c. 145-22], "To His Wife," 2:8

[43] 1 Peter 4:12-13
[44] James 3:13-17, ESV.
[45] Luke 6:43-45, ESV

Chapter Six

[47] Dr. Robert Jones, Lecture at Southeastern Baptist Theological Seminary.
[48] Edward T. Welch, *Addictions: A Banquet in the Grave* (Phillipsburg: P & R Publishing Company, 2001), 32.
[49] Welch, 35.
[50] See Acts 16:14; Romans 10:10; Hebrews 3:12
[51] John Owen, *The Mortification of Sin: A Puritan's View of How to Deal with Sin in Your Life* (Greanies House: Christian Focus Publications, 1996), 51.
[52] John C. Broger, *Self-Confrontation: A Manual for In-Depth Discipleship* (Palm Desert: Biblical Counseling Foundation, 1991), 83.
[53] Josef Solc, *Communicating on the Playing Field* (Maitland: Xulon Press, 2009), 241.
[54] John MacArthur, *Counseling: How to Counsel Biblically* (Nashville, Thomas Nelson Inc., 2005), 83.
[55] MacArthur, 17.

Chapter Seven

[56] See Romans 8:31-39; Galatians 2:20; 1 John 2:16-17.
[57] John C. Broger, *Self-Confrontation: A Manual for In-Depth Discipleship* (Palm Desert: Biblical Counseling

Foundation, 1991), 125.
[58] James 1:12-14, NIV
[59] Romans 6:6-7, NIV
[60] See Romans 8:35-39; 1 Corinthians 10:13; 2 Corinthians 4:7-10; Philippians 4:15-16
[61] John C. Broger, *Self-Confrontation: A Manual for In-Depth Discipleship* (Palm Desert: Biblical Counseling Foundation, 1991), 111.
[62] See Galatians 5:16; Ephesians 3:16-12, 5:18; 2 Timothy 2:22b; Titus 2:11-12
[63] Broger, 111
[64] See 2 Corinthians 5:9; Ephesians 4:1; Colossians 3:17
[65] Romans 12:2
[66] See Romans 6:11-14; Philippians 2:12-13; Colossians 3:5-17
[67] See Romans 8:35-39; 1 Corinthians 10:13; 2 Corinthians 4:7-10; Philippians 4:15-16

Chapter Nine

[68] John M. Frame, *Worship in Spirit and Truth: A Refreshing Study of the Principles and Practice of Biblical Worship* (Phillipsburg, P&R Publishing, 1996), 89.
[69] See 2 Timothy 4:16-17; Hebrews 4:12; Psalm 1:1-2; 119:50, 92; 2 Timothy 3:15-17; 2 Peter 1;3, 19-21; Luke 2:35; Hebrews 4:12-13; Psalm 73:25-28; Romans 11:36; 1 Corinthians 10:31; 1 John 1:3-4 Psalm 19
[70] John C. Broger, *Self-Confrontation: A Manual for In-Depth Discipleship* (Palm Desert: Biblical Counseling

Foundation, 1991), 85.

[71] Frame, 103.

[72] Frame, 81

[73] Colin Marshall and Tony Payne, *The Trellis and the Vine: The Ministry Mind-Shift that Changes Everything* (Kingsford: Matthias Media, 2009), 42-43.

[74] John MacArthur, *Counseling: How to Counsel Biblically* (Nashville, Thomas Nelson Inc., 2005), 114.

[75] Broger, 101.

[76] See Deuteronomy 16:13-15; Psalm 9:2, 33:21, 43:4, 92:1-4; 2 Corinthians 6:1-10; Psalm 16:11; Nehemiah 8:10

[77] David Powlison, "Pride: Be Still My Soul." *The Journal of Biblical Counseling,* V. 18, no. 3 (Spring 2000), 5.

[78] John Ortberg, *The Life You've Always Wanted*. (Grand Rapids: Zondervan, 1997), 59

Chapter Ten

[79] J.I. Packer, *Knowing God.* (Downers Grove: InterVaristy Press, 1973), 132.

[80] 1 Peter 5:10, NIV

Made in the USA
Charleston, SC
21 September 2014